T0266102

No Family is Perfect

No Family is Perfect

A Guide to Embracing the Messy Reality

LUCY BLAKE

WELBECK

Published by Welbeck
An imprint of Welbeck Non-Fiction Limited,
part of Welbeck Publishing Group.
20 Mortimer Street,
London W1T 3JW

First published by Welbeck in 2022

Copyright © Lucy Blake, 2022

Lucy Blake has asserted her right under the Copyright, Designs and Patents Act,
1988, to be identified as Author of this work.

All rights reserved. No part of this publication may be reproduced,
stored in a retrieval system, or transmitted in any form or by any means,
electronically, mechanical, photocopying, recording or otherwise, without
the prior permission of the copyright owners and the publishers.

A CIP catalogue record for this book is available from the British Library

ISBN
Hardback – 9781787396807
Trade Paperback – 9781787396814
eBook – 9781787396821

Typeset by seagulls.net
Printed and bound in the UK.

10 9 8 7 6 5 4 3 2 1

Every reasonable effort has been made to trace copyright holders of
material produced in this book, but if any have been inadvertently
overlooked the publishers would be glad to hear from them.

www.welbeckpublishing.com

I dedicate this book to anyone who has ever felt like they are outside, looking in.

"*No Family is Perfect* is an original contribution to family research and writing. Through interviews and research reviews, Dr Lucy Blake examines the many aspects of family life and addresses the many ways that family relationships can be close or strained. She helps the reader de-romanticize the notion of family, and in doing so, helps us to see how common conflict, ambivalence, even estrangement occur in families. While this is a book that will be useful in academic settings, it is helpful to anyone interested in learning more about their own families. I highly recommend it."

DR JOSHUA COLEMAN

Senior Fellow, Council on Contemporary Families

Author of *Rules of Estrangement: Why Adult Children Cut Ties and How to Heal the Conflict*

"Lucy Blake's *No Family is Perfect* provides a fresh context for exploring issues that engage us throughout our lives. "Embrace the messiness," she enjoins, as we ask key questions about what it means to be a good parent, a good child, a good sibling. The book approaches families across many dimensions – closeness, conflict, estrangement, understanding and love, and puts many usually omitted issues under the spotlight, such as how adult children negotiate care of their parents, the effect of estrangement on both parent and child, and the role of sibling relationships in mental health. Correcting both idealization and demonization, *No Family is Perfect* will change how we think and write about families."

TERRI APTER

Author of *Difficult Mothers* and *The Sister Knot*

"A wonderfully optimistic and original book. I enjoyed reading it, and especially appreciated the conclusion that there's no such thing as a normal family; all families are confronted with their own problems at some point, albeit some more than others. No Family is Perfect is extremely reassuring, and readers will find nuggets that are particularly helpful to them. It also addresses unexpected and important questions, such as what does a good child do? I think that this will resonate with many people, particularly the growing number who find themselves caring for ageing parents, and help them to feel less guilt."

PROFESSOR SUSAN GOLOMBOK

Professor of Family Research, Director of the Centre for Family Research at the University of Cambridge

Author of *We Are Family: What Really Matters for Parents and Children*

Contents

*Over the past two hundred years the meaning of family has been radically transformed from a group of people one lives **with** in the here and now to an imagined entity we live **by** through either a remembered past or a dreamed of future.*

John Gillis, 'Our Imagined Families:
The Myths and Rituals We Live By'[1]

one

Why I embraced the messiness of family life, and you should too

*An ounce of blood is worth
more than a pound of friendship.*

Spanish proverb

The way I thought families should be

Growing up, I thought I knew how a family should be. I absorbed messages about families in different ways. They were in the films and television that I watched and the books that I read. They were in the adverts that I saw and the messages written on the mother's and father's day cards at our local shop. These messages knitted together into a story – the family story – which became the blueprint of how I thought a family should be. For a long time, it was the story that I compared my family against. For a long time, it was the lens through which I judged the lives of my friends and my peers.

The family story was a harsh one, full of judgements of right and wrong. Living within the family story was good; falling outside of it was bad. If you lived within the permitted storylines, you gained the prestige of being "sorted": of having your life perceived by others as being "on track". If you had the shame of living outside of its permitted plotlines, you were the opposite of sorted: you were lost, drifting, or the odd one out.

For me, for many years, the family story went like this:

The family is the cornerstone of society. If families are strong, communities and societies will thrive. Nothing in life is as important as family.

Family should come before the acquisition of wealth and the achievement of personal goals. Those who put anything before and above their families have got their priorities out of order. They will be lonely and unfulfilled. Success is meaningless without a family to share it with.

Family are those people who are tied together by genes, marriage and parenthood. They are the people in our lives with whom we have legally recognized rights, responsibilities, duties and entitlements. We may care deeply about those with whom we lack these ties that bind – we can say that they are like family. But they cannot turn off our life support. They will not be there in times of challenge. Blood is thicker than water. In times of test, family is best.

Family is sacred. The bonds between family members are so close, dependable and important that relationships with friends, neighbours and colleagues do not and cannot come close. Family is love. And not just any kind of love: the unconditional kind. There is nothing you can do and nothing you can say that will unravel the love between family members.

Family is a sanctuary from the ups and downs of everyday life. Family is a safety net. There will always be someone who can give you a roof over your head. There will always be someone who cares about you and wants to know how you are.

Mothers are the beating heart of the family. There is no force on earth that is as strong as a mother's love for her child. And there is no one more worthy of praise than the dedicated dad. If a mother is the heart of the family, the father is the spine. Those who are not parents will know little of sacrifice. They will never know the kind of love that a parent has for a child. They will only know half-loves. They will only live half-lives.

There is no greater gift than a dutiful daughter or a loyal son. Those who are parents will look into their children's eyes and think: My sacrifices were worth it. My choices were the right choices. Those who are parents will have someone to care for them as they grow old. Those without children will face old age alone. No one will care for them or about them.

Those who have a sibling have a friend for life. They will share that special knowing and secret humour that is unique to brothers and sisters. "Only children" will be lonely. They will never know what it is to have a friend from infancy to childhood, adolescence to adulthood, older age to death.

Although there is nothing quite like family, it's not always perfect. Sometimes there will be disagreements and tensions between family members. An unkind word spoken here; a thoughtless comment there. But these ruptures can be repaired with communication, understanding and time; they can – and should – be forgiven. We should let bygones be bygones, because life is short and there is nothing as important as family.

Those who live in unhappy families are the pieces of the puzzle that do not fit. Those who have painful experiences of family life are broken. There must be a reason for their experience of rejection, disappointment or pain. They must be from weak families. Broken families. Chaotic families. They must be bad apples, falling from rotten trees.

The broken ones deserve our pity, but family is redemptive. Those who are broken can be fixed. But if they don't try to mend the gift that they have broken, then they will reap what they sow. Because when it comes to family, there is no act that is beyond forgiveness. Whether we are in the family story or outside of it is entirely in our own hands. If you're good enough and if you're worthy enough, you can belong.

How my job changed the way that I think about families

The way that I thought about families started to shift when I became a family researcher. In my early twenties, I found myself travelling around the UK with a tape recorder, a selection of children's toys and a video camera in my bag. For a decade I worked at the Centre for Family Research at the University of Cambridge, interviewing parents and children in the kinds of families that are not often shown on our screens. I talked to parents who had conceived their children using donor sperm or eggs. I spoke to children who were growing up with two fathers or two mothers. I met with families from the posh, leafy streets of capital cities and those from the rolling hills of rural communities.

I then moved to the Children, Young People and Families research team at Edge Hill University in the north-west of England. I conducted online surveys and interviewed parents over the phone. I travelled to community centres, children's hospitals and cafes to meet parents and their children and find out more about their lives and relationships. I interviewed parents who were raising children with disabilities, chronic illnesses and additional needs, whose children often require care at all hours of the day and the night.

For the past few years, my research has focused on estrangement. I have spoken with adults from around the UK who have shared with me their experience of having a relationship with a parent, sibling or adult child that is characterized by negativity and distance. I have spent many hours scouring books, academic papers and responses to surveys to try and understand how common family estrangement is, why it happens and how it affects people's lives.

In speaking to people about family estrangement, at lectures, with colleagues and around my friends' dinner tables, I have noted something else: that the feelings that commonly arise when people discuss estrangement – specifically, those of shame, pain and isolation – are also common to those who wouldn't categorize themselves as being estranged. These feelings often ring true for those whose families have been affected by substance abuse, or those who are navigating the fractures that can accompany divorce. I am not saying that we are all the same; these kinds of experiences affect people's lives and their relationships in different ways and to different extents. But what I am saying is this: when it comes to the perfect plotlines of the family story, many people feel like they are outside, looking in.

I have learnt that family relationships present themselves in many different ways. I have been offered hundreds of cups of tea and many, many biscuits. I have sometimes been invited to stay for dinner or to share a glass of wine in the sun. The parents in these families have shared with me their joys and their pain, their triumphs and their challenges. The children in these families have told me about their daily lives and their pets. And the stories that parents and children have shared with me have changed me. They have opened my eyes, challenged my assumptions and expanded my heart.

Learning about other people's families has also led me to reflect on my own. Growing up, I didn't know that research was a job that people did to earn a living, so it certainly wasn't planned. But I was always interested in people. I wanted to understand why the people around me did what they did and said what they said.

Fragile memories of family are familiar to me. A teacher at school once asked my classmates and I to draw our family tree, and all I could think to include were those who lived under the roof of my family home. The names of my grandparents, aunts, uncles and cousins were blurry and unclear, so I left those branches bare.

At some point, I started daydreaming about a different kind of family. I imagined myself as a member of a multigenerational cast of aunts, uncles, grandparents and cousins who were both loveable and loving. There would be some minor irritations between family members, but these would be light and amusing, rarely disrupting the flow of laughter around the dining table in the enormous house lit up with hundreds of twinkly Christmas lights. My fantasy family was a heavy-handed rip-off of the 1995 film *While You Were Sleeping*, starring Sandra Bullock as my namesake, Lucy.

At the time that I was daydreaming of this alternative, fantasy family, I was unaware of the complexities and intricacies of my own. I was unaware that my family tree contained branches that had been weathered by mental health problems, poverty, estrangements and untimely deaths. I was unaware that there were branches that had been strengthened by supportive relationships, a commitment to change and a drive towards a better life.

Whereas as a child I had little say over who drifted in and out of my family tree, as an adult I have taken more control over the shaping of its branches. My current understanding of family is broad: I share a genetic relationship and history with some of the members of my family and with others I do not. I have chosen to create and invest in relationships with family members, friends and colleagues by whom I feel valued. These relationships change as we enter new stages of our lives. Sometimes this growth is painful. Sometimes it's beautiful. It is most often both.

How I'm going to try and change the way that you think about families

This is not a book about how we can improve our family relationships. There will be no eight-step plans to family bliss and contentment. It will not argue that our relationships should look and function in a certain way. In this book I will be sharing those lessons that have broadened my understanding of family. These are the lessons that have allowed me to leave behind the black-and-white family story and to enter into the multicoloured, messy, complex reality of family relationships as they actually are. They are the lessons that have allowed me to develop a kinder voice in my head when I think about family. My hope in sharing what I have learnt is that it might bring a gentleness and curiosity to the way that you think about family too.

In this book, I have drawn on my experience of having been a family researcher for over a decade. In particular, I will share what I have learnt from my research on family estrangement. Studying relationships that some describe as broken can shed light on what it is that we think these relationships should look like when they are intact. I will also draw on research on family relationships more broadly, although this book isn't intended to be a textbook that diligently catalogues every development in the fields of research relating to parents, children and siblings. Instead, what I have done is rely on thorough reviews of the research in these areas that have been published in the past 10 years. And I have described those studies that I think are particularly enlightening or relevant to the way that we think about families.

In addition to interviewing psychologists, which is my own field of training and study, I have spoken with experts who work in disciplines that are different to my own. They have generously given me their time, and I share their insights and expertise with gratitude. I have spoken to the heads of charities and non-profits who work tirelessly to change the way that we think about families. And I have also interviewed those who have a broad range of personal experiences when it comes to family relationships who have graciously shared their stories with me. I have changed their names and certain details to protect their anonymity, but the hearts of their stories remain the same.

I have chosen to explore those family relationships that are expected to be lifelong, supportive and safe: those between parents, siblings and children. I have chosen these relationships due to the weight of the assumptions that surround them. Without doubt, other kinds of relationships are as meaningful and important, in spite of being undervalued and overlooked. But the main focus of this book is to challenge the myths that are at the heart of the family story, in which parents, children and siblings play a starring role.

I use the words "parents", "siblings" and "children" broadly, with an appreciation of the fact that the reality behind them is often complex. Although we often assume that these family members have lived under the same roof, share a genetic connection to one another and have a shared history or culture to draw from, this is not true for all. These relationships might look and feel a different way in families in which parents have separated and re-partnered. They might also look and feel different in families in which parents have conceived their children using assisted reproductive technologies or created their families through adoption or fostering. As much as I have tried to draw on a diverse range of family experiences throughout this book, it is a challenging task to capture the diversity of family life.

And although the experiences of the people I have talked to are diverse, they have mostly lived and worked in the UK, North America or Europe. The studies that I have drawn from have likewise mostly comprised samples of people who have been described as living in WEIRD societies, which is an acronym used to refer to those societies that are Western, educated, industrialized, rich and democratic. The lessons that I share will therefore mostly be applicable to and reflective of the family story that is told in countries that are described as Western, developed or rich.

There is, without doubt, a subjectivity that runs through the pages of this book. Although I have drawn on the most rigorous research available and spoken with experts in different fields, the lessons that I share in this book are the ones that I have personally found most helpful in understanding family relationships: both other people's families and my own. In this way, these lessons are my own personal map for how I think and feel about families. I offer them gently: this book is intended to start conversations rather than to end them.

Changing how we think about families

My understanding of family changed slowly, taking many, many years. Rather than going in a straight line, my learning about family has built up in layers. Often, I gained a layer of knowledge in a lecture theatre, or in chatting with a colleague over a slice of cake. At other times, a participant in a study shared something with me that shifted my thinking, or I stumbled across a paper written decades ago that resonated deeply.

The lessons about families that I most value have been hard-won. The call in this book to resist the singular, shaming family story is far from new. For decades, academics, feminists and activists have pointed out the ways in which the family is often a place of oppression in which inequalities are magnified. And yet, the family story persists.

Many of the stories that we grew up with do not serve us as adults. Stories about "the one" will likely lead us astray if we enter into a romantic relationship expecting that just one person can fulfil all of our needs for the rest of our lives. And like those stories about "the one", the family story is particularly resilient.

When it comes to family, unpicking what is myth from what is reality involves swimming against the tide. Messages about perfect, happy families are all around us. Images of selfless mothers and devoted dads are evoked in the speeches of politicians and religious leaders in countries around the world. Images of happy families saturate our media, adverts and social media platforms. And we start receiving these messages about how a family should be from a young age. They are in the pages of children's books and in the images of much-loved cartoons.

Changing how we think about families also requires engaging with facts about difficult realities, like that of abuse, which occurs more commonly than many would like to believe. At first, I found some of the facts and figures that I share in this book to be shocking, almost unbelievable, despite just under a decade of studying psychology under my belt. And at times I still struggle to take on board those lessons that are in direct opposition to the fairytale of family that I have grown up with.

Changing how we think about family can also be hard because family is a topic that we can all relate to, whether we have ongoing, active relationships with the members of our family or not. I have found that when I am doing family research – whether that is reading a paper, interviewing a parent or writing about family relationships – I will inevitably reflect on my own experiences of family life. And after giving a lecture or presentation on my research, it is not uncommon for people to ask me questions like, "Do you think that I'm estranged?" And there will be times when personal reflection is more welcome than others.

For many, acknowledging that there are difficulties in a family relationship might be too painful. The tendency to deny or minimize the more painful experiences of family relationships is a common one. One way of avoiding pain is to idealize our family relationships; whether we are conscious of it or not, it can be easier to think of the family as being perfect than to think of it as being real. Throughout the chapters of this book, these tendencies towards denial or avoidance will be explored gently and with curiosity.

And finally, it can be hard to talk about family in a tidy, focused, narrow way, because family is a topic that is broad and expansive. The feelings that arise when we talk about family can be hard to constrain or tame. Because when we talk about family, we are talking about love, ambivalence, hate, joy, loyalty, betrayal, duty, disappointment and obligation. We are travelling through time, from childhood to adolescence to adulthood, and we are travelling across generations.

Regardless of whether I succeed or fail in changing or challenging how you think about family, I am grateful that you have picked up this book. There is so much to gain from reflecting on the way we think and talk about families, and there is no better time to do so than now.

Why we need to talk about families in a different way

The way that we think and talk about families is always changing. Storylines that were once forbidden and seen as a threat to tradition are now becoming a part of it. For example, I grew up in the UK at a time when it was illegal for teachers to talk about same-sex relationships in schools because it was thought that to do so would be to promote them. Jump forward three decades, and I have celebrated as my friends have married and had children with their same-sex partners.

There are also places where complex, hidden experiences of family relationships are explored in depth. There are, and always have been, places of reprieve. These complex narratives about family relationships are incredibly valuable because they affirm a vital truth: that when it comes to family relationships, those who have experienced challenges, or anything other than love and joy, are not alone.

The ways that we receive messages about families are also changing. I can see them lurking in the click-bait headlines of the media that I consume and in the images that I scroll through in my social media feeds. The ability to distinguish between an advertisement and a photo of a genuine family experience is harder than ever.

But there is still a long way to go. On our screens we rarely see portrayals of those families in which brothers and sisters haven't spoken in decades. We rarely see those families in which parents do not know where their sons or daughters live. Celebrities in the media are singled out and shamed for their experiences of estrangement; their family relationships are presented as a source of speculation and scandal.

The more mundane experiences of family life are likewise hidden from view, because when it comes to family, some things can be said out loud and some things cannot. Parents are allowed to say that they are tired, but they must always be grateful. Siblings can talk fondly about games that they used to play as children, but they cannot share the reflection that if they met their sibling for the first time today, they would probably not be friends. These less palatable experiences of family life stay out of sight. In this way, we rarely witness another person's genuine, authentic family life. We see the outward-facing family; we rarely see what goes on behind the scenes. We see the performance of family, over and over again.

So while the family story has changed, in many ways it remains the same. Some versions of the family story might be more progressive than they have been in the past, but it is still a story that separates us. It is still a harsh tale that encourages us to categorize people as either good or bad. It is a story according to which you can assign worthiness: either you are living within the parameters of the family story and approved of, or you are living outside of it, and shamed for doing so.

It is time to embrace the complexity and diversity of how families are in real life. It is time to acknowledge that family relationships involve a range of experiences and emotions that change over time. And it is time to appreciate that when it comes to family relationships, no two look the same.

We need to think and talk about families in a different way. Because contrary to the images of happy, healthy, functioning families that we see all around us, those who have a wider range of experiences when it comes to family relationships are not alone. People who have experienced challenge, hardship and heartbreak in their families are not other people. They are not those we do not know or have not met. They are our partners, friends, neighbours and colleagues. They are our schoolteachers, accountants, policymakers and cleaners. They are our bus drivers, cashiers, dentists and doctors. They are you and me. They are us.

My job has been an unexpected gift. Writing this book has been more than an academic endeavour; it has been an opportunity to learn to navigate the fragilities and the strengths of my family tree with kindness. I have started to let go of the way things might have been and to embrace what is. I have learnt to appreciate the love that I have been fortunate to have both given and received, even though at times it hasn't looked or felt the way I thought it should. And I have softened into the acknowledgement that idealized, elevated images of significant relationships do not come close to the beauty and the pain of those that are real.

While this is true for me, my work has taught me that we all have different experiences of family life and family relationships. There is no one single story of what family is or what family means. It is time to explore the messiness, diversity and complexity of family relationships and to do so without shame or judgement. It is time to do so with kindness.

two

What does a "normal" family relationship look like?

An average family situation in our society today is one in which people maintain a distant and formal relationship with the families of origin, returning home for duty visits at infrequent intervals.

Professor Murray Bowen,
Theory in the practice of psychotherapy.

According to the family story, parents love their children unconditionally, siblings are there for one another through thick and thin, and sons and daughters are their parents' best friends and confidants. This is the family that is served to us in advertising and saturates our social media feeds; the parents, children and siblings in these families look happy, healthy and content.

So what does a "normal" family relationship actually look like? Is a relationship with a parent, child or sibling that is anything less than warm and supportive a problem that needs to be fixed, or a worthy focus of optimization? When it comes to family relationships, what is it exactly that we should be striving for?

After considering these questions, the chapter will then move on to explore what it is that a "normal" childhood looks like. Are most people's childhoods safe and secure, with only a minority experiencing heartache or challenge? Or are experiences of adversity, like divorce, mental health problems, abusive relationships and violence in the home, more common than we are often led to believe?

This chapter will then consider the extent to which relationships between family members are lifelong. It will ask, how often do relationships between parents and children break down? And why does this happen? And finally, we will explore why talking about family relationships, especially the more challenging experiences that we might have had, can be so hard.

Are most relationships close and supportive?

Growing up, if you had asked me to describe a "normal" relationship between adult family members, I probably would have used words like "close" and "loving". I thought of these qualities as being the default settings of family relationships and that those that weren't in alignment with these qualities would be less common. Interestingly, "close" and "loving" are not the words I would have used to describe the relationships in the branches of my own family tree. Instead, I have often thought of these relationships as being a mixed bag, ranging from those that are active, warm and supportive, to those that are passive, distant and fractious, with some swinging between these different states. But rather than thinking of this as being typical, I had thought of my family as being different from other people's families. So what is it exactly that a "normal" relationship looks like between family members in adulthood?

At first, the studies that I found suggested that most people have regular contact with the members of their family. For example, in a study of approximately 37,000 people in Germany, researchers collected data for over 15 years and concluded that most people visit their family more than once a month but less than once a week.[3]

However, studies that set out to explore specific family relationships in greater depth tell a slightly different story, and most studies that have done so have focused on the relationship between parents and their adult children. Researchers have asked parents and children about many different aspects of their relationship, including: how close they feel to one another; how often conflict arises in their relationship; whether they live near one another; how often they meet up in person or communicate over the phone; the extent to which they give and receive practical, financial and emotional support to and from one another; and whether they share the same values. And, last but not least, they have explored the extent to which parents' and children's expectations of what they think their relationships *should* look like matches up with the reality of the relationship.

In collecting this kind of data from parents and children, studies in the United States,[4] Europe[5] and China[6] have found the same thing: that there is no one "normal" or typical relationship between parents and their adult children. Instead, researchers have identified a range of different kinds or types of relationships. One research group who studied parent–child relationships in the United States found that there were five different types of relationships, which they assigned the following labels: "tight-knit", "sociable", "intimate but distant", "obligatory" and "detached". They explained: "none of the types constitute a majority of relationships or represent a 'typical' relationship"[7]

As well as learning that there is no one "normal" or typical relationship between parents and children, I have been surprised to learn that a substantial proportion are what researchers sometimes refer to as "inactive". For example, the authors of one study analyzed data from 27,500 parents in 11 European countries and found that approximately a third had relationships with their adult children that were "autonomous"; they did not live near one another, they had little contact, and they engaged in few exchanges of support.[5] Likewise, in a recent study conducted in the United States, researchers analyzed the quality of approximately 2,000 relationships between parents and their adult children: 30 per cent were those in which levels of contact were low, as were exchanges of support between parents and their children.[8]

I was also interested to learn that the more active relationships that parents and children have with one another differ in significant ways. For example, in the American study described above, 70 per cent of relationships were active in terms of contact and exchanges of support, yet they differed in their quality. For example, the most common kind of active relationship – making up 29 per cent of the sample – were those in which there were high levels of both positive and negative emotions alongside one another, which researchers refer to as being "ambivalent". The next most common kind of active relationship was one that some might think of as an ideal, in which positivity was high and negativity was low; these relationships made up 28 per cent of the sample.

I have found the findings of these studies to be fascinating, and I have come away from reading them with three main takeaways: firstly, that many parents and children do not have the active and engaged relationships that we often see depicted on our screens, characterized by daily phone calls, exchanges of money in times of need, or lifts to hospital appointments; secondly, that while there are parents and children who enjoy relationships that are high in positive emotions and low in negative emotions, they are not "the norm"; and thirdly, that it is common for relationships to be characterized by positive and negative emotions alongside one another.

My ideas about what it is that a "normal" family relationship looks like have therefore changed: I can now appreciate that – despite the messages that I have grown up with and continue to be bombarded with – there is no such thing. And the mixed bag of relationships in the branches of my own family tree no longer seem so unusual after all. Perhaps my family is more like other people's families than I thought?

What does a "normal" childhood look like?

Just as I had grown up thinking that the default settings of family relationships were those of warmth and closeness, I had assumed that most people's childhoods were times of worry-free play and exploration. The narratives of the family story depict families as being places of safety and security, so I had assumed that it was only a minority of children who would experience intense stress or hardship in their families. But what does a "normal" childhood actually look like?

The idea that it is only a minority of children who experience hardship quickly evaporated when I started to read the research on adverse childhood experiences, or "ACEs" for short, which is a term that refers to negative events that take place before a child turns 18. This body of research emerged in the late 1990s when a group of researchers in the US sent a survey to thousands of adults asking them about their health and their experiences of the following events in childhood: abuse; violence against their mother; and having a household member who abused substances, had a mental illness, had been suicidal or had been imprisoned. They found that experiences of ACEs were common, that they often clustered together and that the number of ACEs that people had experienced was significantly related to numerous risk factors for the leading causes of death decades later.[9]

Since the late 1990s, a vast, sophisticated body of research on adversity has been conducted in countries all over the world. One group of researchers looked at the findings of 37 studies, in which data were analyzed from approximately 254,000 people. They found that just under 60 per cent reported at least one ACE and just over 10 per cent reported at least four ACEs.[10] They found that those with four or more ACEs were at increased risk of a wide range of negative outcomes including: physical inactivity, being overweight or obese, having diabetes, smoking, poor self-rated health, cancer, heart disease, respiratory disease, sexual risk-taking, mental health problems, heavy or problematic alcohol use, problematic drug use and interpersonal and self-directed violence.

Far from being a small problem affecting the few, the effect of ACEs on various health outcomes has been estimated to have had an annual cost in 2019 of $748 billion in North America and $581 billion in Europe.[11] And research on adversity is a field that is very much alive and growing. In addition to the classic or traditional adverse experiences that I've described above, researchers have since added other ACEs to the list, including growing up in foster care, bullying, the death of a parent or caregiver, separation due to deportation, serious medical procedures or illness, neighbourhood violence and discrimination.[12]

ACEs have been described by researchers as "the most intense sources of stress that children can be exposed to".[12] Another term that we might hear commonly is that of "trauma". In his book *The Body Keeps the Score: Mind, Brain and Body in the Transformation of Trauma*, one of the world's leading experts on trauma, Professor Bessel van der Kolk, describes how trauma is by definition "unbearable and intolerable" and can affect people's ability to engage in intimate relationships.[13] In the very first line of his book, he explains that even if we don't have personal experience of trauma in childhood, we know and love people who have. Professor Van der Kolk writes: "One does not have to be a combat soldier, or visit a refugee camp in Syria or the Congo to encounter trauma. Trauma happens to us, our friends, our families, and our neighbours."

One of the most important lessons that I have learnt from the research on adversity and trauma is that these experiences are far from rare. Many children know what it is to worry about a parent who seems unhappy, distressed or unable to cope with daily life. Many children worry about their parents' safety in relationships that are marked by violence and intimidation. And many children do not feel that they are safe, cared for and respected by their parents 24 hours a day.

I have also learnt that these experiences have the *potential* to have a negative impact on children's development and their later health and well-being. The word "potential" is an important one, because while it is true that experiencing multiple ACEs is associated with an increased risk for poor mental and physical health later in life, researchers are clear: "multiple ACEs do not mean that poor outcomes are inevitable".[14]

People's experiences of adversity differ: some experience one ACE, others experience many. Some endure adversity for many years, others experience ACEs for a short period of time. Some experience adversity from a very young age, others in adolescence. Just as experiences of

31

trauma differ, so too do the resources that people have to draw on. Some will have a vast network of family members, friends, and teachers to turn to for help and guidance, whereas others will have little in the way of meaningful, supportive relationships on which to draw.

It is also true that trauma and adversity do not only present people with setbacks. For example, the authors of a recent book explain that these kinds of experiences can present people with opportunities for growth. They write: "Posttraumatic growth does not deny the distress associated with highly challenging experiences at the time, and at certain times after. The evidence supporting posttraumatic growth does, however, demonstrate the unique capacity for many people to learn and grow from extreme adversity".[15]

I have found that the words of poets can be helpful in thinking of how some of the most challenging experiences can affect our lives in different ways. For example, in writing about his childhood in the care system in the UK, the author and poet Lemn Sissay writes: "I am not defined by my scars but by the incredible ability to heal".[16] Likewise, in her poem "The Uses of Sorrow", Mary Oliver suggests that there can be gifts to be found in among the dark experiences of difficult relationships:[17]

(In my sleep I dreamed this poem)
Someone I loved once gave me
a box full of darkness.
It took me years to understand
that this, too, was a gift.

This body of research has led me to think about the events and circum-stances in my own family tree through a different lens. I can see more clearly the challenges that have weathered the branches of my family tree, just as I can appreciate those relationships and resources that have supported its stability and growth. Ultimately, I can appreciate the complex messages that come out of this body of work: that the events of our past matter, but they do not have to dictate our future. But the main lesson that I have learnt is this: that although I had once thought that a "normal" childhood is one of unconditional love and worry-free exploration, this is more a myth than it is a reality.

Why do family relationships break down?

When I first became interested in family estrangement, there was little in the way of published research on the topic. The experience was rarely, if ever, acknowledged in the academic papers that I read, the talks that I attended or the books that I studied. In the press, a celebrity's estrangement from a family member was presented as being rare. And outside of work, few people I knew talked about estrangement. Everywhere I looked, family estrangement seemed to be presented as an anomaly and a taboo, breaking the unwritten rule that relationships between parents, children and siblings are life-long. I was therefore eager to know: Is estrangement between family members rare? And why does it happen?

Although there is no one accepted definition of estrangement, most researchers and clinicians would agree that this term refers to more than a distant relationship. Relationships between family members in which there is little contact are not that uncommon, and they can also have different qualities: whereas some are warm, others are characterized by negativity and have a legacy of conflict. Generally speaking, it is the latter that researchers think of as estrangement.

Just as researchers are developing definitions of estrangement, they are also starting to get a picture of how common it is. In

2014, the charity Stand Alone, which supports people experiencing estrangement, commissioned a nationally representative study of approximately 2,000 people in the UK to explore how common it is.[18] Eight per cent of people surveyed reported that they themselves had cut contact with a family member, indicating that at least 5 million people in the UK have cut contact with a member of their family due to a breakdown in the relationship.

We are also starting to understand why it is that some relationships become estranged. Clinical psychologist Dr Joshua Coleman has recently published *The Rules of Estrangement: Why Adult Children Cut Ties and How to Heal the Conflict*.[19] In this book Dr Coleman draws on his many years of experience in running a practice that focuses on family estrangement. He also draws on his own experience of having been estranged from his daughter, which he describes as having been incredibly painful. Having resolved the estrangement with his daughter, he is now dedicated to helping parents, children and siblings who find themselves in this position. I asked Dr Coleman what kind of parents and children he saw most often in his clinical practice. He replied:

Divorce seems to be one of the more common causes of estrangement that I see in my clinical work. It can provide the opportunity for one parent to poison the child against the other parent. It can bring new people into the child's life with whom they have to compete for love or affection. Even if the parents manage it well, it can cause the children to see one parent as more at fault than the other and then blame that parent for breaking up the family home.

Another common reason is conflict with a daughter- or son-in-law. Clashes in personality and values are certainly common, as are clashes over sexuality, gender identity and religion, with parents typically being more religious and devout than their children. Then there's mental illness, either on the part of the parent or the adult child. In the US, political differences also appear to be an increasingly common cause.

Dr Coleman's experience in working therapeutically with people who are estranged from a family member is both rare and valuable. Another source of insight into the causes of estrangement are studies that set out to explore the experiences of people who identify as being estranged or as having created distance from a family member due to a negative relationship. One researcher whose work has been incredibly valuable in shedding light on the experiences of sons and daughters in this position is Professor Kristina Scharp an expert in Communications Studies at the University of Washington. I asked Professor Scharp to tell me why it was that she thought children made this choice. She explained:

I would say that adult children choose to initiate distance from a parent due to a pretty large range of some sort of abusive behaviour, whether that's emotional, verbal, physical, sexual or parental substance abuse. Or another factor that contributes to estrangement is where parents and children have wildly diverging values and beliefs as they pertain to things like sexuality and religion – those things that people hold very fundamental to their personal identities. And it can be some kind of intersection of all of that, because estrangement often happens in these on-again off-again patterns, so sometimes the first reason isn't the same as the second reason. It can be difficult to figure out the cause of an estrangement actually because it's not always one thing.

Similar themes have emerged from research conducted in Australia by Dr Kylie Agllias, who recently published the book *Family Estrangement: A Matter of Perspective*.[20] A number of the sons and daughters who have taken part in her in-depth studies have described their mother or father as engaging in inadequate or sub-standard parenting. They have explained that their desire for a distant relationship stems from feeling like their parents are demanding and critical, and feeling like they had to be an emotional and physical support system or crutch for their parent while they were growing up.

These insights from research can help us understand the factors that contribute to estrangement. And in addition to research findings, clinicians, therapists and counsellors who work with those who experience estrangement are sometimes influenced by the theories of the family therapist Professor Murray Bowen. Professor Bowen described the creation of physical and emotional distance between family members as "cutoff".[2]

According to his theory, cutoff is more likely to happen in relationships in which anxiety is high, and when family members struggle to recognize and manage their emotions and to think clearly under stress. His theory also predicts that cutoff is more likely to happen when family members find it hard to remain in connection with one another while maintaining a clearly defined sense of self; or, in other words, when family members perceive differences in opinion, memories, perspectives or beliefs to be a personal attack or affront.

In her book, *The Dance of Intimacy: A Woman's Guide to Courageous Acts of Change in Key Relationships*, author and psychotherapist Dr Harriet Lerner draws upon Professor Bowen's theories as to what cutoff is and why it happens. In doing so, she explains that, while we might think that those who are estranged lack feelings for one another, the opposite is in fact true. She explains: "It is important to understand that distance and cutoff between family members have nothing to do with an absence of feeling, or a lack of love or concern. Distance and cutoff are simply ways of managing anxiety. Rather than reflecting a lack of feeling, they reflect an intensity of feeling".[21]

Although research on family estrangement is fairly small, we are starting to understand more about why and how often it occurs. And the lessons that I have learnt about estrangement in the past few years were not what I was expecting. I wasn't expecting to find that it was so common: that while estrangement doesn't affect the majority of relationships, it is far from a rare occurrence. I also didn't expect to find that the relationships between family members break down for such a vast range of reasons. With these lessons in mind, the media reports about a celebrity's estrangement no longer seem so scandalous or shocking. And neither do the estrangements that have occurred in my own family tree.

Why don't we talk – really talk – about family relationships?

I spend a lot of time talking about family relationships. I talk about them at work, when I'm collecting data or giving lectures to students. And I talk about them outside of work, because family small talk is a common, inevitable feature of daily life. People want to know who you spend time with and what you're going to spend time doing, especially around the holidays. People talk about family like they talk about the weather. But why is it that we rarely talk about family in a meaningful way? Why is it that we feel that we can only talk about those experiences that are positive?

What I have come to understand is that, although it is common, family small talk can be stressful. One reason why this topic of conversation can be distressing is that the more challenging aspects of family relationships are steeped in stigma, at the heart of which is a separation between "us", the "normal" majority, and "them", the stigmatized minority. Let's take one ACE as an example – growing up with a parent with a mental health problem. In countries around the world, it is estimated that between 15 and 23 per cent of children live with a parent with a mental health problem.[22] Yet despite the fact that it is far from rare, it is no wonder that both parents and their children might want to keep this information private. A recent review found that the stereotypes most associated with mental health problems are that those who are affected by them are responsible for them, incompetent, weak in character, dangerous or dependent.[23] Few parents – or their children – would want other people to see them through this lens.

Just as there is stigma surrounding mental health problems, there is stigma surrounding family estrangement. Professor Kristina Scharp at the University of Washington is interested in how people talk about family relationships, and family estrangement in particular. I asked Professor Scharp to explain why it is that family small talk can be so hard for those who are estranged from a family member. She explained:

Most people perceive family to be a safe topic because everyone has a family. And I think if you come from a really happy family it might not occur to you that not everybody comes from a happy family. One of the most common conceptions is that families are these lifelong, obligatory relationships, so when you experience something counter to those cultural norms, that can be something that pervades your whole life. Because even if you wanted the distance, and even if you were able to successfully accomplish the distance, you still live within a culture where that is unheard of, at best, or unacceptable. Any time you violate a social norm that is held really dearly by society, you are going to be punished. If you choose not to have a relationship with your family, no one thinks you're eccentric – they think something is probably wrong with you, even when that might not be the case in the slightest.

Professor Scharp's response allowed me to understand that few people will want their colleagues, friends or partners to judge them in this way. No one wants to be thought of as abnormal. And within my own discipline of psychology, I have learnt something else too, which is that even thinking about difficult family experiences can be challenging, let alone sharing those thoughts with other people.

I learnt this lesson through studying attachment theory, an influential theory at the heart of which is the notion that our early childhood experiences go on to shape the quality of our relationships throughout the course of our lives. Professor Miriam Steele is the Co-Director of the Center for Attachment Research at the New School in New York and a leading clinician and researcher in attachment theory. I am incredibly grateful to have been trained by Professor Steele and her team in how to study family relationships through the lens of attachment theory. I reached out to Professor Steele to clarify why it is that thinking and talking about our family relationships can be so difficult. She explained:

I think it can be hard to understand your childhood because it might be painful and we all want to protect ourselves from the pain of being rejected and feelings of loss. If you go back to the writings of one of the founders of attachment theory, John Bowlby, and his original thinking about this in the 1930s, he wrote about something he called "defensive exclusion". That when things are difficult to process, you tuck them away because to think about them would be too painful.

Relationships that have some challenges but are overall good enough, they're not so hard to engage with and come to terms with. But the painful ones are the difficult ones. Those realities like, "I was unloved", or "my parents loved work more than me, or drugs more than me, or other relationships more than me", are so painful. We often have an inability to tolerate mental pain. We don't like it.

From an evolutionary perspective we come into the world needing that love, so there are ways that children will do almost anything to protect the image of their parents in their mind, like believing that their parents' lack of love was their own fault because they are unlovable. And not only is thinking about the past sometimes painful, but it can be hard work, which some people don't really want to do. You can get by with denial, but it only works so far. The by-product of not thinking about or dealing with difficult emotions and memories is that they still exert an influence on our lives.

What I have learnt, is that talking about family relationships often necessitates an ability to acknowledge and tolerate pain. And I have also learnt that, as well as denying its existence, people hide from or minimize pain by creating fantasies of perfection. I have been surprised to learn that someone speaking about a parent as being entirely without fault or limitation – as being superhuman – is not necessarily an indication that that person has had a perfect relationship with their parent, or a perfect childhood. Professor Steele explained:

> As a clinician and a researcher, if someone tells me "my childhood was perfect", that can set alarm bells ringing, as this can be another way in which people avoid difficult feelings and experiences. Idealizing parents and thinking of them as perfect, without flaws, can be a way of keeping things superficial so that we don't have to engage with reality.
>
> Relationships can look very good from the outside, but actually the people in them might not be getting much out of them. So, for example, someone might make it look to the world "Oh, my mother, she was wonderful, she was out there and helping everybody, she was so warm, she was really involved in charity work". But this might be a way of avoiding the reality that "actually, she wasn't that great towards me. For me, she wasn't there at all". It's really quite amazing the way the human brain can function to make it look to the world as if there is no pain there.

In speaking with Professor Steele, I have come to understand that in talking about family relationships in an authentic or vulnerable way, not only do we potentially open ourselves up to judgement, but we might need to acknowledge, and potentially feel, pain. With these lessons in mind, I now understand why it is that we tend to only really talk about family relationships in a positive, if not idyllic and idealistic, way. I can also appreciate that when we talk about family like we talk about the weather, we are only really inviting stories of sunny days. And that in talking about family in this way, the idyllic narratives of the family story are the ones that we most often hear, and the only ones that we might feel comfortable in telling. The more nuanced, complex reality of family life and family relationships remains hidden, and the family story lives on.

The importance of knowing
what you don't know

These lessons that I have learnt have allowed me to appreciate that there is no "normal" kind of relationship between parents and children in adulthood. I can now actively resist judging my own family relationships against those of the perfect, imaginary families that I see on my social media feeds. And I can reassure myself that when I experience the push and pull of positive and negative emotions in a family relationship, that they are not a problem in need of fixing, or an indicator of deficiency. Instead, I can reassure myself they are an expected, natural part of being in a relationship with a family member.

And in learning these lessons, an important illusion has been shattered, which is that, unless I am told otherwise, other people have experienced a safe, secure childhood, free from adversity. I have also learnt to appreciate that adversities live in the branches of my own family tree, even if they are rarely mentioned or labelled as such. And what I now know is that these events and circumstances are what make my family tree similar to other people's family trees, rather than different from them.

When I keep these lessons in mind, the world is no longer neatly split into "good" and "bad" families. Not only do the harsh, judgemental narratives of the family story start to fade, but they start to feel woefully inadequate. In my intention to both understand and extend kindness to myself and others, it not only becomes easier to walk away from the judgemental narratives of the family story – it becomes vital to do so.

What I now know is that before I speak with someone I have absolutely *no* ability to guess what kind of challenges and strengths exist in their families. I likewise have no ability to guess what they might have experienced or endured in the past. It doesn't matter what car is in their drive or how wide their smiles might be; not even their selection of biscuits can give it away. No matter how people present themselves, no matter how "picture perfect" their families might appear to be, until someone decides to share their world with me, I genuinely have no idea what they have experienced in their family relationships.

Aware that I know so little, I try to resist making assumptions about other people's lives and their family relationships. I try to keep in mind that although I might sometimes think that I know few people who have been affected by adversity in childhood, or estrangement from a family member in adulthood, without a shadow of a doubt this is not true. The people who I love, work with, teach, learn from and pass in the street will have encountered a diverse range of experiences in their family relationships.

With these lessons in mind, I talk about family in a different way than I used to. I do not assume the students that I teach and the colleagues that I work with have active, supportive relationships with their parents or their children. And I'm more likely to tread lightly around family talk, with compassion and an awareness that, for many different reasons, family is not necessarily an easy topic of conversation to navigate.

three

Raising young children: what makes a "good" parent?

What mother doesn't have to dance between her own needs and tugs, her child's cries, her dreams, his desires? What mother doesn't come at this most complex of projects with a handicap of some sort, somewhere? You tell me, what mother is perfect? To my daughter I say this: I am sorry. I am so far from being able to give you all that you need, but know one thing. You have my whole effort. You have my whole heart, for whatever it's worth. I love you.

Lauren Slater, *Playing House: Notes of a Reluctant Mother*[24]

Parenthood is a defining feature of our lives. Whether we are a parent or not, we have probably thought about – or been asked to explain – why our lives look the way that they do. But it isn't always easy to define what it is to be a parent. Do we have to give birth to or "father" a child? Or is it more important to be at the parenting coalface – comforting a crying child or taking care of a child who is sick?

More complex still is the question of what it means to be a "good" parent. We see examples of how a mother or father should be – or shouldn't be – in our own families, and in the families of our friends and neighbours. We receive messages about what a "good" parent should do in the television series and films that we watch, the books that we read to our children and our social media accounts. Increasingly, being a "good" mother or father is a tall order: nothing less than perfect selflessness and dedication will do.

So what exactly is "good" parenting, and to what extent is self-lessness and relentless dedication necessary for children to flourish? And should mothers and fathers be held to the same or to different standards? This chapter will then consider child abuse: is it rare? How does it affect children's lives? And why do we rarely talk about it?

Are "good" parents those
who love their children?

I used to think of parenting as being simple: "good" parents are those who love their children. This is a message that I hear people say often, and it is certainly one that I have said myself. So what exactly is "good" parenting? And does it just come down to love?

Some researchers look at what it is that parents say; they interview them and ask them to answer questions about their child. Others look at what it is that parents do: they observe parents and children interacting with one another at their home, in a lab or online. And increasingly, researchers are interested in what children think and feel, which they explore in a number of creative ways. For decades, researchers have used these different tools to study how parenting affects children's well-being, making conclusions about what kind of parenting behaviours are associated with positive outcomes for children, such as an ability to form friendships, engage in behaviours like helping and sharing, or good mental health.

In studying parents who are raising young children, researchers describe specific behaviours – the things that parents do – as falling into two broad categories: positive and negative. Positive parenting behaviours are those that are warm, responsive, encouraging, accepting and involved. Discipline involves clear and consistent limit-setting – children know what it is that they can or cannot do. On the other side of the coin, negative parenting is inconsistent, over-reactive, controlling and harsh. The rules about what it is that children can and can't do change, so they are never quite sure how their parent will react if and when they cross the line.

Unsurprisingly, a recent review of parenting research summarizes that positive parenting is associated with good outcomes for children's development and negative parenting with poorer outcomes.[25] However, it is specific parenting behaviours that are categorized as positive and negative, not parents themselves. For example, a parent might find it relatively easy to show warmth and affection to their child, but they might find it less easy to set clear and consistent limits in terms of their behaviour. Researchers have little interest in whether parents engage in positive behaviour across the spectrum, achieving a "perfect" score. Because despite the cultural messages that we receive about perfect, selfless, dedicated parenting, engaging in positive parenting behaviours at all hours of every day is neither possible nor necessary for a warm and loving relationship to develop between a parent and a child. When thinking about the way that parents interact with their children when they are young infants, a recent paper written by leading psychologists from around the world stressed that a record of 100 per cent perfection isn't possible. They explain: "even the most sensitive and responsive of caregivers necessarily 'tune out' from time to time".[26]

This distinction between positive and negative parenting behaviours is a helpful one; we get an idea of what kind of behaviours are associated with good outcomes for children and vice versa. But there is another important part of the puzzle when it comes to determining what constitutes "good" parenting, which is how children feel, and, specifically, whether children feel loved. For example, in one paper, the findings of 551 studies were analyzed: and the authors concluded that, across cultures, ethnicities and geographical locations, children who felt accepted by their mothers and fathers were more likely to be psychologically well-adjusted than those who felt rejected by them.[27] Simply put, children who feel loved, cared for and appreciated fare better in life compared to those children who feel unloved. Determining what is good parenting therefore not only depends on what parents do, but how their children feel.

And there's another important factor to consider too. Psychologists who study parenting in countries around the world argue that we need to acknowledge the rules or expectations of a particular culture when it comes to thinking about what it is that "good" parents do. The theory is that children compare their parents' behaviour to what it is that they see other parents doing. So, for example, if a parent yells at a child and that child thinks of yelling as being unusual or rare, they will feel rejected by their parent. However, if they think of yelling as a "normal" parenting behaviour, they will be less likely to take it personally, and more likely to assume that their parents are simply acting how parents are supposed to act.

Another complication in thinking about parenting is that beliefs and expectations about what it is that "good" parents do change over time. One review of parenting research argued that in countries that are described as Western, developed or rich, parenting has become "intensive".[28] Central to intensive parenting is an assumption of parental determinism: that how children fare in life is a direct result of their parents' behaviours and efforts.

But "good" parenting has not always been thought of or presented in this way. For example, in one US study, a researcher looked at the ways that mothers were depicted in adverts in magazines over the past few decades. In the 1950s, the perfect mother was presented as diligently caring for her home, husband and children, in that order. But by the 1990s, the portrayal had shifted; adverts had begun to depict a "good" mother as a woman whose children are her priority, whom she cares for by following the advice given to her by experts such as doctors, nutritionists and therapists.[29]

Beliefs about what it is that "good" parents do also change among child development experts. During my PhD, I was enormously fortunate to be supervised by Professor Susan Golombok, the Director of the Centre for Family Research at the University of Cambridge. For more than four decades, Professor Golombok has studied children's development in those families that couldn't exist or were hidden from society 40 years ago, such as those created by assisted reproductive technologies and those headed by two mothers or two fathers. Her studies and books have consistently explored the question "What matters?" when it comes to children's well-being, with the findings of her studies influencing family policy in countries around the world. I asked Professor Golombok how her understanding of parenting and what really matters for children's development has changed over time. She replied:

When I started out studying children's development in lesbian mother families in the mid-1970s, it was widely assumed, by just about everybody, that a parent's sexual orientation would influence their children's development. But my research, and the research of others in the field, showed that this wasn't the case. The things that people used to think really mattered for children's well-being – the number of parents in the family, the gender of the parents, the sexual orientation of parents, and the biological relatedness of parents to their children – seem to matter much less than we used to think they did. What the research on new family forms has shown is that what really counts for children is the quality of children's relationships with their parents and the social environment in which the family is situated.

For both child development experts and the public more generally, beliefs about what it is that "good" parents do change over time. And so too has the way that I think about parenting. Because what I know now is that "good" parenting isn't just about whether and to what extent a parent loves their child. Rather, what I have learnt is, firstly, that "good" parenting refers to what it is that parents do when they interact with their child; secondly, that "good" parenting can be determined by how children feel and, specifically, whether they feel loved; and thirdly, that parenting is considered "good" or "bad" depending on the way that a parent's behaviours are perceived in their particular culture. What I have learnt is that trying to capture an image of what it is that a "good" parent does requires more than a photograph taken by a single camera. Rather, capturing what it is that "good" parents do requires an exhibition of images that have been taken from different perspectives, using a range of filters and lenses.

What does "good" parenting come down to?

Back when I used to think that parenting was simple – that "good" parents are those who love their children – it seemed logical to assume that "good" parenting came down to dedication. Seen through this lens, parenting is a virtue: all that really matters is the extent to which a parent is selfless, dedicated and determined. But to what extent is this true? Are we right to value and praise those parents who try the hardest and do the most? When it comes to parenting, are we right to celebrate sacrifice, and selflessness?

What I have come to understand is that these qualities are far from the minds of experts who study parenting and child development. Instead, they study a wide range of factors that are often depicted in diagrams that show numerous boxes that are linked together with a dizzying array of arrows. I'll explain a simplified version of one of

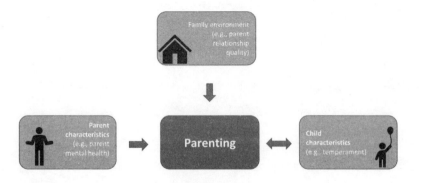

these diagrams above, and in doing so I'll draw on a review of parenting research that have been conducted in the past three decades.[25]

When thinking about parenting, researchers consider the characteristics of the parent. These include a parent's personality, their childhood experiences and their mental health. For example, studies have found that depressed parents are more likely to engage in negative parenting compared with parents who are not depressed. This difference in parenting isn't about a parent's love, or lack of love, for their child. Rather, as depression affects the way that people think and feel – for example, involving rumination on negative thoughts – the theory is that a depressed parent will have less capacity to focus on their children's perspectives and to respond to their needs appropriately. However, the relationship between parenting and depression is far from simple. For example, the age of the child during the parent's depressive episode is important, as is the severity and the duration of the depressive episode and the financial resources that are available to the parents in the family.

Then researchers consider the characteristics of the child. Some have focused on children's temperament, which refers to an infant's tendency to react to stressful environments with irritability, anger, sadness or fear. Parents of infants who react to stress in this way have been found to be more likely to engage in higher levels of negative parenting. But again, this field of research is a complex one and many questions remain unanswered. For example, researchers question whether it is a parent's perception of their infant's temperament or their child's temperament itself that explains this pattern. And again, the level of financial resources that are available to parents, and the level of support that they receive from friends and family matter too: those with fewer resources and lower levels of support might find it harder to respond to their infant's challenging nature in positive ways. Thinking about a child's temperament in this way is not intended to blame an infant for how they are treated by a parent. One of the most influential psychologists to have studied children's development, Professor Mary Ainsworth, explained the imbalance in the parent-child relationship in this way: *"adults have needs and responsibilities. Infants only have needs"*.[30]

Next, researchers think about the family environment, such as the level of social support that the parents in the family have to draw on. In two-parent families, researchers also take the quality of the parents' relationship with one another into consideration. Parents who engage in frequent, intense conflicts with their partners that lack resolution have been found to be more likely to engage in negative parenting. Again, this isn't because they love their children less, but rather because intense, prolonged conflict can lead to parents feeling irritable and drained, reducing their capacity to focus on and respond to their children's needs sensitively.

And all of these factors are influenced by what researchers refer to as "socio-economic status" or SES, which is typically measured by a parent's level of education or employment. However, the authors of the review I have drawn on stress that it is important to consider SES in a comprehensive way. They explain: "SES goes far beyond 'amount of dollars' or 'amount of education' that parents have attained.

Low-SES is likely associated with a host of other factors that impact parenting, such as neighborhood quality, access to quality childcare, availability of developmentally-appropriate toys and learning materials in the home, stability of caregivers over time, household chaos, access to high quality and affordable food, and exposure to toxins".

Although they are complicated, I have found models of parenting and child development to be helpful. When people tell me about their family relationships and childhood experiences, I find myself mentally sketching diagrams of boxes in my mind, mapping the various resources that parents have been able to draw on and the challenges that they have faced.

To bring these models of parenting to life it can help to step into the daily lives of mothers and fathers in different kinds of families. One kind of family that we rarely see on our screens are those in which children experience chronic illnesses that are longstanding or life-threatening, such as cancer or traumatic brain injury or inflammatory bowel diseases. Unsurprisingly, researchers have found that compared to parents whose children are well, parents of children with chronic illness are more likely to experience poor mental health and financial stressors.[31] If we think of parenting in terms of the model described above, we could therefore predict that parenting would differ in families in which children have a chronic illness compared to families in which children do not.

One group of researchers set out to address this very question, pulling together the findings of 325 studies.[32] While they found that the relationships between parents and their children were less positive if a child had a chronic illness, they stressed that the size of this difference was small and that this pattern varied depending on the nature and severity of the child's illness. They concluded: "most families with a child with chronic physical illness adapt well with regard to the parent–child relationship".

Psychological research can feel judgemental – as if so-called experts are pointing fingers and assigning blame. But when it is conducted sensitively and with compassion, parenting research allows us to understand the many different factors that influence the way that a mother or a father engages in parenting. And this understanding can then be used to inform interventions to support the parents and the children in these families.

Although parents whose children with a chronic illness have additional challenges to manage, being a parent of a child with very complex health care needs takes parenting to a different level altogether. To understand more about the daily lives of the parents in these families, I reached out to Professor Bernie Carter, an expert in Children's Nursing at Edge Hill University in the north-west of England. I worked alongside Professor Carter for five years, benefitting from her many years of experience of studying families in which parents care for their children at home. She explained:

Being a parent to a child with complex health care needs is emotionally and physically draining, because even when they've got support workers coming into their homes, they never feel off duty. The high-level care that these parents give is relentless and few of us can imagine how they manage this 24/7. Most of us, even when we've done a really long, full-on day, can go home and relax and sleep. We're not waiting for our child's oxygen alarm to beep in the bedroom next to us. We don't have to get up three times in the night, every night, to give them their medication.

Besides the pressure of the parents having to give expert clinical care to their child, there's little awareness of how often their lives – as a parent, a partnership or as a family – are both narrowed as well as enriched. What is certain is that their choices are limited. One parent usually must give up paid work and become the full-time carer. The person who goes to paid work may lose their career aspirations as they want to be close to home, or maybe they have to work longer hours to cover the costs associated with their child's needs. Everything shifts.

But it's definitely not all doom and gloom. The ways that parents, children and siblings in these families can cope and adapt is remarkable, especially given that this is not what they signed up for as parents. Despite the fact that parents act as their child's carer, they perceive themselves to be a parent first and foremost. I don't think anybody has got a real clue as to how tough it is for these parents; even small amounts of additional support can be like winning a prize."

Professor Carter's vivid description brings to life what it might be like to be a parent of a child who needs a lot of support. Research on parenting in different kinds of families is growing, and our understanding of the ways that parenting impacts child development is always evolving. But what I have learnt is that when it comes to what makes a "good" mother or a "good" father, it makes little sense to value dedication and grit or to prize selflessness. Instead, what I have taken from the extensive research on parenting and child development is three main messages: firstly, that many different factors impact how a mother or father parents their child; secondly, that the contexts in which parents raise their children matter; and thirdly, that all families fit within these diagrams: there is no family in which "good" parenting comes down to dedication alone.

Does mother know best?

Having been born in the UK during the 1980s, most of the films and television that I grew up with presented family life in a particular way: mothers were the primary caregivers who were in charge and fathers were second in command. Fathers were active and involved in raising their young children, but in many different aspects of family life they were simply not as important as mothers. But to what extent does this pattern reflect men and women's natural instincts and abilities?

The first lesson I have learnt is that messages about what it is that mothers and fathers do are pervasive. For example, in an analysis of children's books published in the United States from 1902 to 2000, researchers found a consistent pattern across time: whereas mothers were portrayed as nurturing and caring for children, fathers were depicted as working outside of the home.[33] It seems that this message is still a potent one today. In a recent analysis of articles in American parenting magazines, fathers were mostly presented as the primary breadwinner and as a secondary parent in relation to mothers.[34]

The assumption that mothers are the best suited to being a child's primary caregiver is evident not just in children's books and parenting magazines, but in family policy. One important area where mothers are treated as the best or most natural caregiver of young children is parental leave following the birth of a child. In 2015, researchers compared parental leave policies in Australia, Canada, Ireland, New Zealand, the UK and the United States. They confirmed that parental leave policies were primarily aimed at mothers rather than fathers, with maternity leave usually being longer than any other kind of parental leave.[35] Another area of life where mothers are assumed to be the best or most natural caregivers of young children is how parenting is organized or divided following divorce. A recent review of research in this area identified that there has been a shift in practice.[36] Whereas mothers typically provided primary childcare after a parental separation or divorce, joint physical custody, in which a child lives with each parent for at least 25–50 per cent of the time after separation or divorce, is becoming increasingly common in many Western societies, although these arrangements are still far from the default setting.

Messages about what it is that mothers and fathers do are all around us, not just in our media and our books, but in family policy and legislation. So what then do we know of "nature" – are mothers actually better suited to childcare than fathers? Are family policies that favour mothers based on assumptions, or on accurate knowledge about mothers' and fathers' abilities?

For decades, researchers have set out to address these questions. Since the 1970s, researchers have studied the nature and the quality of fathers' relationships with their children. They have filmed fathers interacting with their infants in laboratories and in their homes. They have asked fathers to fill in surveys and to answer various questions in interview settings. They have examined fathers' hormone levels before and after their children have been born.

In reviewing these studies, Professor Michael Lamb, Emeritus Professor in Psychology at the University of Cambridge, reached the following conclusion: "new mothers and fathers are equivalently competent (or incompetent) at parenting, with most parenting skills learned 'on the job'. Because women in this society on average spend more time on the job, they often become more skillful at it over time. However, this disparity in parenting skills simply reflects women's greater experience and greater opportunities to learn rather than a biologically given capacity".[37] He likewise concluded that the more recent research that has examined fathers' hormone levels has found that both men and women are physically prepared for, and changed by, parenting.

The message that men and women are equally competent at parenting can also be found in research on families that are headed by fathers. In countries like the UK and United States, there are a rising number of single-father and two-father families in which children grow up without a mother in the home. The fathers in these families have typically created their families by adoption, fostering or assisted reproductive technologies. In her latest book, *We are Family: What Really Matters for Parents and Children*, Professor Susan Golombok summarizes the findings of her studies of children's development in families headed by two fathers in this way: "Our research suggests that fathers who take responsibility for the upbringing of their children can be just as competent as mothers, and that children can flourish in the absence of a mother".[38]

These research findings are ones that are close to many people's hearts. Not only do people find them interesting and validating, but they understand that they can be used to influence and implement change in policies and legislation. One father who is aware of the power of research on this topic is Josh Levs, a UN Gender Champion who wants workplaces to build policies that support fathers to be equal caregivers in corporations, organizations and universities all over the world. Josh was a fact checker at CNN when his daughter was born prematurely. He found that as a father, he was only entitled to two weeks of parental leave, whereas mothers and adoptive parents were entitled to 10 weeks. This led Josh to request equal parental leave and when his request was denied, he filed a legal complaint against Time Warner, CNN's parent company. Josh's pursuit for equality for fathers was a successful one – a year later, the company changed their parental leave policy, improving father's access to leave following the birth of a child.

Josh aims to take the messages from research on parenting and actively embed them within workplace policies, which he describes as having been developed during the "Mad Men" era, referring to the TV series which depicts family life in the United States in the 1950s, with fathers typically working outside of the home and mothers staying at home to raise children. Josh explains that "the issue of male caregiving has been in the shadows for too long and we need to shine a light on it". He believes that we should not be surprised that in countries where it is available, fathers do not take their full entitlement of paternity leave. He explains: "Men face derision, demotions and even loss of their jobs when they make family a priority".

As well as fighting for equality in workplaces, Josh believes that it is important to model equality at home. He explained how he aims to practise what he preaches when it comes to his own family:

I think with kids what you do is always more impactful than what you say, so my wife and I try to model gender equality to our kids. We talk about it a lot as well. We call out any examples of sexism that we notice and we discuss it. I remember when our daughter was born, sometimes I'd be taking care of her and my eldest son who was seven at the time, he would start telling me what to do: "No daddy don't do it like that". I looked at him and said, "Wait a second, do you think that men are less capable than women of taking care of babies?" And he looked at me and he said, "No I tell mommy what to do too." Which we thought was really funny. So we watch out for it and we demonstrate at home that yes, mothers and fathers can do everything and it's totally natural and normal to come up with your own way to balance all of these responsibilities as a couple.

Even though Josh has the findings of decades' worth of social science research on his side, thinking of men and women as equally competent caregivers of young children requires swimming against the tide. Not only has the message that men are less capable at raising young children been planted in our minds from a young age, but mothers and fathers are treated differently in courts of law and by policymakers in countries around the world. But without a doubt, the findings from many years of studies that have explored this question are clear: mothers and fathers are equally capable at parenting.

What about abuse?

For a long time, I thought that child abuse was rare. This was how it was presented in the media, and I don't remember it being raised as a topic of discussion in lessons at my school. Child abuse was only touched on briefly in my four years of undergraduate and five years of postgraduate training in Psychology. So how often do parents abuse their children? And what exactly does the word "abuse" mean?

I wasn't anticipating the definition of child abuse to be so broad. This is a complex area – just as definitions of "good" parenting vary between cultures and generations, so too do definitions of abuse. Many researchers use the definitions proposed by an influential report published by the World Health Organization following a consultation of 27 experts from around the world, in which the following distinctions were made.[39]

Emotional abuse was defined as the failure to provide a child with a supportive environment, including a relationship with an available parent or parent figure with whom a child can develop: "a full range of emotional and social competencies". Emotional abuse was also described as encompassing acts such as the restriction of movement, patterns of belittling, denigrating, scapegoating, threatening, scaring, discriminating, ridiculing or other kinds of hostile or rejecting treatment. Physical abuse was defined as the infliction of actual or potential physical harm by a parent which is reasonably within the control of a parent. Neglect was defined as a caregiver's failure to provide for the development of the child in terms of their health, education, emotional development, nutrition, shelter and safe living conditions, in the context of resources that are available to the parent or caregiver. And finally, sexual abuse was defined as the involvement of children in sexual activity that they do not understand, are unable to give informed consent to and for which they are not developmentally prepared: the activity is also intended to gratify or satisfy the needs of the abuser.

As well as being surprised to learn that child abuse covers such a wide range of behaviours, or lack of behaviours, I was not expecting to find that it was so common. In one of the most thorough and extensive studies on child abuse to date, a research team analyzed the findings of 244 studies, reporting data from approximately 850,000 individuals.[40] In a paper published in 2015, they concluded that child maltreatment affects the lives of one third of children around the world. They estimated that the prevalence rate of emotional abuse was 36 per cent. The next most prevalent kind of abuse was physical, which was estimated to affect 23 per cent of children, which was followed by neglect: the world prevalence rate of emotional neglect was estimated to be 18 per cent and physical neglect to be 16 per cent. Finally, the world prevalence rate of sexual abuse was estimated to be 13 per cent.

Given that the scale of child abuse is so large, it is particularly important to understand how these experiences can impact people's lives. One research team looked at the findings of approximately 2,500 studies that included data from half a million people who had been maltreated as children.[41] They concluded that, across the course of a person's life, all forms of child abuse were associated with negative outcomes in physical health, mental health and various elements of children's development, for example, negatively impacting children's attainment in school, their language development and their ability to form relationships with other people.

However, experiences of abuse do not always or necessarily result in negative outcomes across the course of a person's life. People's experiences of abuse vary, in terms of its nature, its severity, the age at which it occurred, as well as its duration and frequency. People's access to support also varies, both in childhood and in adulthood. Whereas some might have a rich network of supportive relationships to draw from, others might have little. Although child abuse presents a potential risk to survivor's mental and physical well-being, there is no one way that abuse affects people's lives.

Given that child abuse is common, and that its impact on development and health is far-reaching, I wanted to understand why we talk about this topic so rarely. To find an answer, I turned to Professor Michael Lamb. Michael's research examines how testimony is obtained from children who have experienced abuse, and his work has resulted in significant change in the ways in which children are interviewed by authorities in countries around the world. He explained:

When it comes to those who have experienced abuse, a lot of people don't disclose because they are afraid of the consequences. Especially for children who are afraid of the consequences of what will happen if the authorities become aware of what's going on and the family breaks up. Then there's embarrassment, and the fear of opening up about very personal, intimate experiences. I think in many cases there's shame, and shame in multiple forms including the fact that, certainly in the case of sexual abuse, it's not at all uncommon for children to feel some degree of culpability; abusers may actively encourage that narrative because the more the child is complicit the less likely there is to be disclosure of the abuse.

And there's the fear of being disbelieved. Especially when the parent has some standing, the immediate response is going to be, "I can't believe that Bob would ever have done that." That's the worst of all possible worlds when you've kept something secret for a long time and get the courage to make a disclosure and then it's your integrity that's challenged rather than that of the abuser. And I think all of those factors are really important. I think that all of those reasons still apply to the fact a lot of cases of abuse are never disclosed and that a considerable number of abused kids don't mention it until adulthood. And even when they do disclose it may only be to the people they trust rather than to any kind of authorities.

Professor Lamb's response opened my eyes to the many reasons why people who have experienced child abuse don't share this information with other people. I then asked him to tell me more about emotional abuse in particular, given that it is the most common kind of abuse that children experience. He explained that, in the world of research, most studies have focused on sexual or physical abuse because these are often specific events, whereas when it comes to emotional abuse, "you have more of a fabric of non-experiences that define the event". He went on to explain:

> Emotional abuse is a combination of things, which includes specific incidents of parents or caregivers calling children names and using rejecting, disparaging or hostile language. But it seems to me that those are probably just the symptoms of something that's much bigger and broader and probably more painful, where it's hard to really put your finger on "it". It has more to do with emotions and feeling that you're not able to get something as much as what you do get. Everybody who works in the field would tell you that as far as effects are concerned, it's the emotional abuse that is most powerful with respect to its impact on children's adjustment.

Professor Lamb's response was helpful in allowing me to appreciate the many reasons why emotional abuse in particular is shrouded in silence. I have come a long way from thinking of child abuse as rare and knowing little about what it actually is. I now understand that abuse doesn't only happen when a parent hits a child, but that there are other kinds of behaviours that have real consequences for children's well-being too, like being belittled or ignored. I also know that all kinds of child abuse are related to negative outcomes across the span of people's lives: that it is not only acts of physical violence that are abusive and harmful to children's development.

I have also learnt that there is no one way that abuse in childhood affects the parent–child relationship. For example, in a study conducted in the United States, researchers asked approximately 3,000 adults if their parents or caregivers did the following when they were growing up: insulted or swore at them; sulked or refused to talk to them; did or said something spiteful; threatened to hit them; smashed or kicked something in anger; kicked, bit or hit them with a fist or object; beat them up; choked, burned or scalded them.[42] They then asked them how they would rate the quality of their relationship with that parent or caregiver as they were growing up. Approximately half (47 per cent) of those who had experienced physical and emotional abuse evaluated the relationship with their parent as being "excellent", "very good", or "good". The authors of this study explained: "some individuals can experience maltreatment and still report a satisfactory relationship with either or both parents … families are complex and dynamic entities whose biographical imprint often forms untidy, complicated storylines".

What I have come to understand is that, while the impact of child abuse on a child's mental and physical health can be negative and long-reaching, abuse does not necessarily mean that parent–child relationships break down. Instead, what the findings of studies like these suggest is that there is no one way that abuse affects the relationships between a parent and a child over time.

However, there are more firm conclusions that we can make about the abuse of children by their parents. And, arguably, the most important lesson that I have learnt is that the abuse of children by their parents is not rare. What I take from these research findings is that you cannot assume that the fact that your friends, family members, colleagues and acquaintances don't talk about abuse means that they haven't experienced it. If we do not have these experiences in our own lives, we will know, love, work with, teach and live alongside people who have.

Is love really all you need?

I once laughed when I interviewed an American father who told me that he was saving for his seven-year-old child's future therapy fund. It was only after the interview that I realized that he probably hadn't been joking, because this father had gone on to articulate his awareness that he could never meet all of his child's needs in the right way and at the right time. He reflected that striving to do so might be an unwise ambition, accepting that rather than being a perfect parent, he was a human being, and as such could only try his best.

I don't think I understood then that some element of failure is an inevitable part of parenthood, or life in general. I probably still believed in that idealized image that a parent could be everything to a child and meet all of their needs, unfailingly. Because when we think about our own parents or parent-like figures, it is tempting, if not inevitable, that we will assign them a score and deliver our verdicts on how we think they did. And it is tempting, when doing so, to compare them to an imaginary parent, who rarely, if ever, puts a step out of place.

The ways that I think about parenting have changed. I now know that, contrary to the messages I receive in the media and on my screen, "good" parenting isn't about selfless, perfect dedication. I now know that perfection is not only unachievable but unnecessary. And I also know that "good" parenting isn't just about the way that parents treat their children, but also about whether their children feel loved and accepted, and to what extent that parent's behaviour is in line with the culture in which they live.

Rather than a parent's love for a child being perfect and timeless, I can now appreciate that the way that parents interact with their children is shaped by circumstance. In gaining this understanding, I have found a softer, kinder place to land when I think about parenting. The labels of "good" and "bad" became inadequate in capturing the messy reality of what it is that mothers and fathers do when they are raising a child. Because the ability of a mother or a father to be a "good" parent does not come down to love alone, nor strength of character; no parent is above or beyond context or their history. The Beatles anthem "All You Need Is Love" is a beautiful one, but the reality is a little more complex when it comes to parenting.

I have also learnt that there are two common messages about parenting that need to be challenged. The first is that mothers are the best or most natural caregivers of young children, because the reality is that mothers and fathers are equally capable of parenting. And the second is that child abuse is rare, because the reality is that child abuse is estimated to affect the lives of a third of children around the world. And a vital first step in understanding family relationships is to talk about them as they actually are, rather than as they could or should be.

four

"Good" parenting when children are grown

Though many of us take pride in how different we are from our parents, we are endlessly sad at how different our children are from us.

Andrew Solomon, *Far from the Tree: Parents, Children and the Search for Identity*[43]

Once you become a parent, there is arguably little that can alter this identity: not the death of a child, nor the removal of a child from your care, nor becoming estranged from a child later in life. Parenthood is an identity that is both life-changing and lifelong. As the authors of a review of studies on parent–child relationships explained, spouses, friends and colleagues might come and go, but "once a parent, always a parent".[44]

This chapter will explore the quality of the relationships between parents and their children when they are adults. In doing so, it will question the extent to which a parent's love for their child is unconditional. Do parents love their children regardless of their successes or failures in life? And what kind of factors make the relationships between parents and their grown children particularly close?

This chapter will then move on to examine how divorce affects the quality of the relationships between parents and their children when they are adults. Do the stresses and the challenges of divorce leave their fingerprints on these relationships over time, or is divorce a common family event from which parents and their children bounce back fairly quickly? And lastly, this chapter will consider the experiences of parents who are estranged from their adult children, which is typically surrounded by stigma and silence. It will therefore explore how the estrangement from a son or a daughter affects parents' lives.

Do parents love their children regardless of their successes and failures in life?

Central to the family story – the way we think families should be – is the notion that a parent's love for a child is unconditional. It therefore shouldn't matter whether a child is considered to be wildly successful or an abject failure: parents should love their child no matter what. But to what extent are these assumptions true? Do parents love their children regardless of what it is that they have achieved, or failed to achieve, in life?

When their grown children experience setbacks and failures in life, sociologists predict that parents will perceive these events (or lack of events) to be an indicator of personal failure: that because their child has failed, they have failed in their job of being a parent. In a review on the relationships between parents and their grown children, the authors explain: "[parents] tend to view their children as extensions of themselves, and their well-being is often tied to their offspring's success as adults".[45]

So to what extent is a parent's worth tied up in their children's lives? As sociologists have predicted, parents have been found to have lower levels of psychological well-being when their children experience certain events in life. For example, in a study of approximately 36,000 parents living in 17 European countries, parents' levels of depression increased when one of their children divorced.[46] However, the country in which parents and children lived mattered: those parents living in countries where divorce is less socially acceptable, like those in southern Europe, experienced a greater increase in depression compared to parents living in Nordic countries, where divorce is more acceptable. The findings of this study suggest that it is not just the events that happen in children's lives that are important, but how these events are perceived in the wider society in which they live.

Having one child who is particularly successful does not seem to detract from the distress caused by the perceived failures of another. For example, in a study conducted in the United States in which data were collected from approximately 600 parents, those who had a least one adult child who experienced a life problem had poorer well-being, even if they perceived their other grown children to be doing well in life. This finding led the authors of this study to conclude that "it may be true that parents are only as happy as their least happy child".[47]

Researchers have also explored how parents feel when their children engage in behaviours that are illegal and pose risks to their health. For example, in one Swedish study, researchers analyzed data from approximately 700 parents who were members of support groups and treatment centres for parents of adult children with drug problems.[48] More than 85 per cent of the parents reported that their child's drug problems had had a negative impact on their lives to a great extent. I spoke with one of the authors of this study, Dr Torkel Richert, at Malmö University in Sweden, to understand how and why a child's drug problems had such a negative impact on parents' lives. He explained:

A child's drug use can affect parents' lives in different ways. It obviously depends on many factors like how long this has been going on for and the severity of the drug problem, but common to almost all parents that I've spoken to is that they experience negative consequences in everyday life as well as feelings of shame and blame. I think the stigma is around parents blaming themselves and asking questions like: Could I have done something different? Is this my fault? Should I have set more limits for my child? I think that also has to do with the view in society that as a parent you have responsibility for your child's health and their well-being even when they are adults.

Having learnt that parents have the tendency to blame themselves for their child's drug problems, I was interested to know to what extent a child's drug abuse affects parents' daily lives and their well-being. Dr Richert explained:

The parents who I have spoken to experience worry, constant worry, about their child's health and their risk of experiencing an overdose, or violence, or exposure to or engagement in criminality. Parents can never really relax because if the phone rings they wonder, Is it the police? Is it the hospital? There's always a feeling that something might happen, all the time.

Parents also experience feelings of powerlessness because they cannot change the situation or help their child in the way that they want to. The parents of grown-up children are in a difficult situation because their children are adults, so their parents can't have contact with social services or authorities to get information about their child because of data protection. So when a child turns 18, nothing changes in the relationship, but legally things change quite a lot, which can present problems.

Dr Richert went on to explain that although both mothers and fathers were affected by their children's drug problems, it was mothers who typically struggled the most:

> We found in one of our studies that mothers are affected to a higher degree than fathers when it comes to shame and guilt and this also has to do with society's view of motherhood. Still, I think women have the bigger responsibility for family life and they get the blame when something goes wrong in the family, so they are seen as having a bigger responsibility. I think they also take a bigger responsibility in general for family and family problems.

Dr Richert's explanation allowed me to understand what sociologists refer to when they talk about "linked lives": that the events that happen in a child's life affect their parents' lives. One research group explained this theory in this way: "an individual's life is embedded within the lives of their family members".[49] It is therefore understandable that when a child is involved in risky and illegal behaviours, this can be a particularly painful experience for their parents that can engulf their daily lives.

It is hard to reach conclusions about a parent's love for a child. But what the findings of these studies suggest is that parents benefit from their children's successes in life, especially when they are in alignment with the expectations and beliefs of the societies in which they live. A child's success is a stamp of approval for parents, confirming to them not only that they did a good job, but that they are a good person. But for parents whose children are experiencing setbacks or whose well-being is at risk, the role of parent can be one of shame, worry and self-doubt, and their children's perceived failures can bring their very worthiness into question.

Why are some parents and children closer than others?

In the family story, the love between parent and child is both enduring and robust. If the snapshots of perfection that saturate social media were to be believed, parents and their grown children in "normal" families enjoy close, supportive, active relationships with one another throughout the course of their lives. But as we have discovered in chapter two of this book, there is no one "normal" relationship between a parent and their grown children: the quality of these relationships varies. So why is it that some of these relationships are particularly close and warm? Is it those parents who were loving, committed and selfless when they raised their children who go on to experience these kinds of relationships later in life?

What I have come to understand is that there are many factors that shape the quality of the relationships between parents and their grown children, many of which are arguably out of the control of parents (and their children). One such factor is gender. Studies that explore the quality of the relationships between parents and their grown children typically find that mothers have closer relationships with their children than fathers. For example, in one US study of approximately 600 parents, mothers had more frequent contact with their adult children and were more likely to be in relationships of mutual support with them compared to fathers.[50]

This pattern is perhaps unsurprising given that in chapter two we explored how the belief that mothers are the most capable parents of young children is common in both popular culture and family policy. Researchers also explain this gender difference in terms of "kin work" or "family work", which refers to the effort that family members make to maintain connections with one another. This includes visiting one another; sending and receiving texts, phone calls, emails, letters and cards; engaging with one another on social media; the organization of virtual or real-life parties or reunions; the coordination of support if a family member falls ill; and the process of sharing information if a family member is diagnosed with a health condition. And for decades, researchers have found that it is the women in the family who are most likely to do this work, which is why women tend to have closer relationships with their adult children than men. For example, in a unique study conducted in Europe, researchers analyzed over three billion phone calls made from a mobile service provider over a seven-month period. From analyzing the patterns of calls that people make, they concluded that women play a more central role in holding together the different generations of the family compared to men.[51]

It is perhaps unsurprising that women are the most likely to do family work. Women tend to be raised to behave in ways that are caring, empathetic, supportive and helpful, so it is therefore to be expected that they take on the role of strengthening relationships between family members. In their book *Burnout: The Secret to Unlocking the Stress Cycle*, Emily and Amelia Nagoski explain the different expectations that we have of women compared to men in the language of "Human Giver Syndrome". They explain: "At the heart of Human Giver Syndrome lies the deeply buried, unspoken assumption that women should give everything, every moment of their lives, every drop of energy, to the care of others".[52]

In addition to gender, studies have found that parents and their children tend to have closer relationships when they share similar principles and morals. For example, in a study conducted in the United States, researchers found that mothers felt closest to their grown children with whom they shared values and that it was these children about whom mothers felt the greatest pride. On the other side of the coin, mothers felt the greatest disappointment in those children who did not share their values.[53] For example, a number of the mothers in the study valued marriage and therefore expressed disappointment when their children had engaged in affairs or ended their marriages. However, it wasn't just a child's marital status that mattered. Some of the mothers in this study expressed disappointment when their children did not live up to the expectations that they had for them, for example, if their daughters had married someone whom the mother considered to be a problematic choice of partner.

In addition to gender and shared values, studies have found that another factor that shapes the quality of the relationships between parents and their grown children is health. For example, in a study of approximately 3,000 Chinese elderly adults living in Chicago, those parents who were in poorer physical health were more likely to have relationships with their adult children that were characterized by high levels of closeness alongside high levels of conflict, which the authors describe as being ambivalent.[4] The authors concluded that "health is an important resource of older immigrants that enables them to better negotiate the ways in which they interact with their children and to engage in a reciprocal rather than dependent relationship".

In addition to these broad factors that shape the quality of the relationships between parents and their children over time, psychologists would no doubt look at the question as to why it is that some parents and children are particularly close through a different lens. Many would predict that those who have the closest relationships in adulthood would be those who had the closest and most positive relationships when children were young. However, they would also acknowledge that these relationships are not set in stone, but rather that they are always changing, especially when children experience common life events like marriage, divorce and parenthood.

The way that parents and children think about their relationships also changes over time. In his book about the Harvard longitudinal study – one of the world's longest follow-up studies of human development – Professor George Vaillant observed that some of the men in the study described their relationships with their parents in very different ways over the course of the study. For example, when he was in his late teens, one participant described his relationship with his mother as having been an affectionate one. However, when the same participant was asked to describe the quality of this relationship six years after he had left home, he described it as having been a miserable one in which he had never felt happy. Professor George Vaillant reflected: "People are complicated; memory, emotion and reality all have their own vicissitudes, and they interact in unpredictable ways".[54]

What I have learnt is that many factors play a part in the extent to which parents and children have close relationships in adulthood, many of which are out of the control of parents and children. Unlike the simplicity of the narratives of the family story, which depict these relationships as static and unchanging, and overwhelmingly positive and close, the reality of these relationships is not so simple or straightforward.

How does divorce affect parents' relationships with their grown children?

Most researchers have tended to focus on the effect of divorce on family relationships when the children in the family are young. But what about the long-term impact of divorce on family relationships over time? Is divorce an event that weakens the relationships between parents and their children in the long run? Or is it an event that family members can bounce back from relatively quickly?

Even though divorce is a common event in family life, it is generally understood to be a stressful one. In a review of research on divorce, Professor Ulrike Zartler, Professor of Family Sociology at the University of Vienna, explains that divorce can have a negative impact on both parents and children.[55] For example, following divorce, parents can find themselves taking sole responsibility for parenting, fighting for custody or losing custody of their children. Whereas the children in the family can find themselves having to deal with ongoing conflict between their parents, having less contact with one parent and potentially having to move to another home or school.

Although these experiences are typically negative ones, not all divorces are the same. For example, Professor Zartler explains that parents have different levels of financial security and varying levels of social support from family and friends from which to draw.

Divorcing couples also vary in their ability and their willingness to communicate with their ex-partner and to engage in raising their children in a collaborative way. Custody arrangements vary, as does the extent to which divorce is stigmatized in a particular country and culture. The takeaway message from this diversity is this: just because a divorce doesn't appear to have long-term detrimental effects in one specific family – such as a family in which parents have vast levels of financial wealth and access to psychological support – this doesn't mean that the parents and the children in another family will experience divorce in the same way. It is also interesting to explore what we know about the impact of divorce on family relationships over time, once the dust from the divorce has settled and the children in the family are adults. Studies conducted in North America and Europe have found that adult children of divorced parents tend to have poorer relationships with their fathers compared to those whose parents have remained married.

So why is it that divorce impacts the relationships between fathers and their children in this way? In a review of research on the relationships between parents and their grown children, Professor Matthijs Kalmijn, Professor of Demography at the Netherlands Interdisciplinary Demographic Institute, offers a number of different explanations as to why these patterns exist. He suggests that children can often feel caught in the middle when parents divorce, which leads them to feel closer to one parent than the other.[56] He also explains that, in divorcing their child's mother, fathers lose the "kin-keeper" of the family, as it is women who typically maintain the relationships between the different members of the family. If fathers do not take on this role, remembering to send birthday cards, make calls and arrange visits, they might find themselves having more distant relationships with their children.

However, rather than following a simple pattern, the impact of divorce on fathers' relationships with their children over time varies. For example, in a study conducted in the Netherlands by Professor Kalmijn, family relationships were compared in two groups: adult children whose parents divorced during childhood and adult children whose parents remained married in childhood. Professor Kalmijn found that the more involved fathers were in the child's life, the better the quality of their relationship with their adult children, regardless of whether parents had divorced or not. He also found that when it comes to the quality of the relationship between fathers and their children, those with higher levels of education were less likely to be impacted negatively by divorce. In explaining this finding, he suggests that fathers with higher levels of education might be more aware of the possible negative effects of divorce on children, or that these fathers could be more skilled in negotiating good parenting arrangements after divorce.[57]

Although divorce tends to weaken the relationship between fathers and their adult children, some might find that their divorce has contributed to the breakdown of this relationship entirely. Divorce is a route to estrangement that clinical psychologist Dr Joshua Coleman is familiar with. In a survey that Dr Coleman conducted of 1,600 parents who were estranged from their child, he told me that approximately 70 per cent identified divorce from their child's mother or father as contributing to the estrangement. I asked Josh why it is that divorce is so prevalent among the parents who come to his clinic, to which he replied: "A lot of the parents I work with going through divorces were loving parents but when they spilt up the kids were like, 'Screw you, you've broken up our family', 'You broke Mum's heart', or 'Dad said you had affairs'. Divorce can cause the child to see the parents as individuals with their own strengths and weaknesses, and less as a family unit that they are a part of."

Although researchers have studied the ways that divorce can weaken relationships between parents and children, Professor Zartler explains that divorce is not a one-time event.[56] Rather, divorce and separation are "step one" in the way that a family changes, and "step two" typically involves the formation of new relationships and the potential break-up of new relationships. And when parents in the family form new relationships, children experience the arrival of step-parents, half-siblings and step-siblings into the family. Researchers acknowledge that it is important to explore parents' and children's relationships in the context of all of these changes in family life, not just the initial divorce.

It seems that the impact of divorce on the relationships between parents and their children can be long-lasting, and that this is especially true for fathers who have not been particularly involved in their children's lives before their divorce. But research also indicates that parents' and children's experiences of divorce vary, and that divorce is often the beginning of change in family relationships, not the end. And while family relationships change, so too does the context in which divorce occurs. In a number of countries, the ways that custody is granted following divorce is changing, with shared custody arrangements becoming more common than in previous generations. Parents also have access to apps that can help facilitate communication with their ex-partner. Like everything to do with family life, the norms and expectations surrounding divorce are always shifting. It is therefore possible that in some contexts, and in some families, the impact of divorce on parents' relationships with their children over time will change.

How does being estranged from a child impact parents' lives?

When I first started to study how family estrangement affects people's lives and relationships, I wasn't exactly sure what I would find. But given that the parental identity is such an important one, and that being a parent is expected to be a lifelong role, I would have expected to find that estrangement from a child would be a negative experience.

Although few studies have explored parents' experiences of estrangement, the main lesson that I have learnt so far is that being estranged from a son or a daughter can be incredibly painful. And one of the reasons why it can be so painful is that it is an isolating experience. For example, in an in-depth study that was conducted by Dr Kylie Agllias in Australia, parents who identified as being estranged from an adult child described sharing their experiences of estrangement with few people, and rarely, due to the fear that they would be judged.[58] This fear of being judged is something that I have heard often when speaking with parents who are in this position. For example, I spoke with one mother, Anne, who told me that she no longer had an active relationship with her two daughters following a divorce from her children's father. She explained that this was an experience in which she felt alone and misunderstood:

Even friends don't really understand. They'll talk to you about it, but there's only a limited time that they're prepared to spend talking about it and then suddenly it's "Well I'm sure they'll come back in time", that kind of thing. Deep down inside I feel, well no, I won't ever get them back, they won't ever come back to me. I just feel empty and totally unsupported and totally alone.

I had a friend visit and her children are just taking their exams at school, and I was telling her about my daughters and their experience of choosing a university and how they drifted away from me. And she said to me – she is very happily married and she's got her two lovely children – that that would never happen to her. I was quite shocked at that comment because when I was at the same point in my life as she is now there is no way that I ever would have thought that my children would drift away from me. Because everything can be seemingly perfect and you can have these goals – and it can all be taken away in the blink of an eye. Everything that you worked for. Everything that you've strived for.

In addition to feeling misunderstood and alone in their experience, the pain of estrangement can be exacerbated by feelings of shame, which tend to be particularly deep and poignant for mothers. In the Australian study of parents who were estranged from a child, Dr Kylie Agllias noted that the mothers in her study had often raised children at a time when motherhood was expected and other identities, like those of being a working professional woman, were unavailable to them. The loss of the role and identity of mother was therefore a particularly significant and painful one. The fact that mothers in particular feel a heightened sense of shame about estrangement is a pattern that Dr Joshua Coleman has also observed in his clinical practice. He explained this pattern in this way:

> What I commonly see is that mothers appear to suffer with the consequences of estrangement more than fathers. What I sometimes say is that 'Mums get sad and dads get mad' and I think that it has something to do with the fact that mothers are never allowed to be off the hook. Mothers don't have the same kind of cultural refuge that dads have; mothers can't say, "Screw them, who needs that, they owe me", because mothers feel like they have to constantly blame themselves and feel like there must be some solution if they only keep trying.

In addition to feelings of isolation and shame, a key feature of estrangement from a child is that of loss of the role and identity of parent, as well as the loss of the relationship itself. Dr Kylie Agllias explains that the parents who took part in her study experienced what researchers often describe as being an ambiguous loss, especially those parents who hope that there will be a possibility of a reconciliation with their child in the future. The shapeless nature of the pain that can accompany this loss was clear when I spoke with one mother, Joanne, who had become estranged from her daughter when she moved out of home around the age of 18. Joanne explained that over the years she had tried taking all kinds of actions in the hope that one day they would reconnect:

Initially, when my daughter moved all her stuff out, I was in a panic. I asked her to write down what it was, because I couldn't absorb it. It was a short letter, but she explained in it that it was an abusive relationship and she needed time to recover. And I didn't know what to do. I seem to remember feeling a combination of numbness and searing pain. My attitude, initially, was to give her time and let her go through it, I thought – she needs to reject me, it's all normal. It's an extreme version, but she'll go through it.

Over the years I've tried all sorts, I've tried texts and phoning the house, phoning her mobile. I've tried giving her loads of space. I'll try anything I can think of. I'll talk to anybody, and I'll listen to anybody who suggests anything because maybe they've thought of something I haven't thought of. I do find ways of finding the occasional bit of information and I do find some comfort in thinking: At least she's alive, she's well.

Maybe she'll reach an age where she's interested in knowing me again, which I hope she does, although maybe she won't. I know with my own mother I had to work through all sorts of complicated emotions, and then eventually I felt, it's either I accept her how she is, with all the difficulties, or I don't have a family. She never once told me she loved me, and I couldn't forgive her when I was younger. But at the end of the day, my mum's love for me wasn't expressed with comfort and cuddles, but every morning my breakfast was on the table, she hand-knitted my clothes, she gave me the thing that she thought was most important – which was religion – that was her love for me. And in her last few years of her life we re-established contact. And maybe that will be the same for me and my daughter.

In listening to parents like Anne and Joanne, we can come to understand that the experience of estrangement is an incredibly painful one. However, it is also true that few studies have set out to explore whether there are any positive outcomes of estrangement from a son or a daughter. Sociologists would predict that this is an unlikely outcome, as many studies have found that parents are typically more invested in the parent–child relationship than their children are. One research team explained the imbalance in the relationship in this way: "Parents view their children as continuations of themselves and thus perceive more positive feelings in this tie, whereas children desire greater independence from parents and are more invested in enhancing differences".[59] It is therefore unsurprising that the loss of this relationship would be a significant blow for parents.

Research on family estrangement is a field that is small yet growing. While we know about those parents who identify as being estranged and who volunteer to take part in studies, we know little about those parents who have initiated estrangement from their adult children, or those for whom pinpointing who initiated the estrangement is more difficult. But what I have taken away from this research is that for parents, being estranged from a son or daughter can be a deeply painful experience, involving feelings of isolation, shame and loss.

A high-stakes relationship

The main lesson that I have learnt about parents' relationships with their grown children is that feelings of tension are to be expected in this relationship. Arguably, a child's successes and failures in life are not just their own, but rather they are an indicator of how well their mother or father fulfilled the prominent, lifelong identity of being a parent. When we are evaluating a parent's value as a human being, a functional, positive family life and a successful child isn't just a nice outcome or the icing on the cake: it can be a mandatory condition of worthiness. No wonder then, that the parent–child relationship can be one that at times feels fraught: it is a high-stakes relationship.

So often in evaluating our family relationships our focus is narrow, up close; we see the strengths and the shortcomings of our family members in granular detail. But the lessons that I have learnt have allowed me to understand that many factors shape the relationships that parents have with their grown children, and that many of these are ones over which parents and children arguably have little control. For example, family relationships are shaped by the expectations that we have about the way that men and women engage in and maintain relationships. Therefore, the question of who sends cards on birthdays and who arranges to see family members in the holidays isn't just a question of who carries out a chore, or an action that is anticipated to bring pleasure: it is a pattern that might well have ramifications for the quality of family relationships for generations to come.

Another broad factor that can shape the relationships between parents and their grown children is that of divorce, especially for fathers who have not been involved in their children's life before the divorce. Although effort is not required in the narratives of the family story, the findings of this research indicate that relationships between parents and their children are not by their very nature loving or enduring, but rather that these are relationships that require continued, active engagement over the courses of parents' and children's lives.

I have also learnt that, for parents, the breakdown of a relationship with a child can be an experience that is extremely painful, isolating and shameful. Mothers and fathers in this situation do not only lose a relationship with their child, but they lose an identity and a role that is highly prized by society. Parenthood is revered, respected, celebrated and admired, but we rarely talk about the more difficult experiences of being a parent over time. Although the family story is an idyllic one, in which we assume that the bonds between parents and children are warm and close, the reality of parent–child relationships over time is a little more complex and varied than the adverts would have us believe.

five

What is it exactly that a "good" child does?

Love is a creative act. When you love someone you create a new world for them. My mother did that for me, and with the progress I made and the things I learned, I came back and created a new world and a new understanding for her.

Trevor Noah, Born a Crime: Stories from a South African Childhood[60]

The expectations of parenthood are high: nothing less than perfection will do. But what kind of expectations do we have about children? Does a "good" child treat their parents with respect and reverence? And when they are adults, do "good" children support their parents and care for them if and when they need it? Or is the role of child more about receiving than it is about giving? Perhaps sons and daughters owe their parents very little, especially if they feel that they were not adequately cared for in childhood.

This chapter will explore what it means to be a "good" child, and in doing so, it will question the age at which children should take on roles of responsibility within their families. Presumably it can't be at the beginning of a child's life: infants are entirely dependent on their parents or caregivers for their survival. Yet despite this vulnerability, babies are not always free from judgements. Family members, friends and strangers often ask a new parent: "Are they a good baby?", implying that there is such thing as a bad baby. So at what age do children's responsibilities start?

This chapter will then explore the motivations of children who care for their parents in older age, when they are more likely to need support with tasks like household chores and practical errands, as well as companionship. Caring for a parent in older age is not a universal experience: many parents will not require care, and if they do, many will not wish for their children to fulfil this role. But caring for a parent is far from a rare experience either. Do those sons and daughters who take on this role do so out of a sense of duty and obligation?

And finally, this chapter will explore the abuse and neglect of parents by their daughters and sons. Given that abuse is entirely absent from the family story, this chapter will consider what elder abuse is, how often it happens and why it is that we rarely talk about it.

How should children treat their parents?

In the model of family that I grew up with, parents were expected to give emotional, financial and practical support to their children, and children were expected to be on the receiving end of the equation. This pattern was expected not just in childhood but in adulthood too, reversing only if parents experienced ill health in older age. So when it comes to the question of what it is that a "good" child does, is the answer – nothing?

In countries that are described as Western, developed or rich, studies have found evidence of the pattern that I have described above: that support typically flows down the generations, from parent to child, only reversing when parents reach older age. For example, in one study that was conducted in the Netherlands, thousands of parents and adult children were asked about the support that they both gave and received in their relationship. The author of the study, Professor Matthijs Kalmijn, found that children were more likely to receive practical and emotional support from their parents until around the age of 75 to 76; at this age, parents became more likely to receive support from their children than to give it to them.[61]

But this pattern is far from universal. Studies conducted in other countries find evidence of the opposite pattern. For example, in one study researchers collected data from approximately 5,500 adult children living in China, Japan, Korea and Taiwan; the children in the study reported giving financial and practical support to their parents rather than the other way around.[62] In these countries, support therefore flows up the generations, from child to parent.

That downwards support is the dominant pattern in some countries, and upwards support is more common in others, is not surprising when we consider the moral principles that shape family relationships in particular cultures. For example, in East Asian societies such as China, Hong Kong, Korea, Japan, Singapore, Taiwan and Vietnam, parent–child relationships are shaped by filial piety.[63] The authors of a recent study have found that, rather than being static or overly simplistic, filial piety is an evolving concept; whereas this principle was once understood to refer to an attitude of deference and obedience to parents, more recently it has come to be understood to encompass feelings of affection for parents and the expectation that children will give their parents emotional support and advice.[64]

In some countries, these principles are enshrined in law. In a bulletin of the World Health Organization, the authors explain that, in the mid-1990s, Bangladesh, China, India and Singapore developed filial-support laws.[65] For example, the 'Maintenance of Parents Act' of 1995 in Singapore details the monthly allowance to be paid by adult children for the maintenance of their parents. Similarly, China's 'Law for the Protection of the Rights and Interests of the Elderly' of 2013 strongly encourages children to consider the health care and social needs of their older relatives. However, rather than demanding strict compliance from adult children, filial support laws are predicated on two conditions. The first is that the parent has a need for support, and the second is that responsibilities should be assigned on the premise of fairness and reciprocity, so those children whose parents abandoned their parental obligations would be relieved of this responsibility.

Another cultural value that shapes family relationships is that of familism, which has been described as being a dominant principle in Hispanic and Latino cultures. In a review of studies that have explored this concept, the authors explain that "familism creates a sense of obligation to take care of one's family, and to take one's family into consideration when making decisions".[66] And these expectations are particularly strong for the women in the family. Professor Roberta Espinoza explains that women's roles in the family are influenced by the cultural value of *marianismo,* which "prescribes dependence, subordination, esponsibility for domestic chores, and selfless devotion".[67] Therefore, for Latina women to be considered to be "good" daughters, they are expected to show selfless devotion to family and to prioritize family needs above their own.

Although I have tried to capture and to simplify the distinct concepts of filial piety and familism, some have described them as overlapping. For example, in a recent review of research in this area, the authors identify a number of beliefs that are common in both cultural value systems, which include: that parents should be treated with honour, respect and obedience; that family members should be loyal to one another; and that family members should support one another, especially in times of need.[64] They also explain that, rather than being unique, "filial piety and familism are concepts that are relevant to all ethnicities, not just the originating ones".

Other researchers have drawn more of a distinction between cultures in which familism and filial piety are dominant and those in which they are not. For example, countries like the UK and the United States are often described as being individualistic, which is to say that the needs of the individual are considered to be more important than the needs of the collective, or in this case, the needs of their family members. Yet this is not to say that there are no expectations in these countries as to what it is that "good" children do. Beliefs about children's obligations to their parents are also shaped by religious principles. For example, in one academic paper, an ordained minister and a professor of law explain that in Jewish, Protestant or Catholic traditions, the fifth commandment, "Honour your father and your mother", refers not just to the acts of caring for a parent, but to a child's intention to do so and their attitude of reverence to their mother and father.[68]

Adult children living in countries that are described as being individualistic might also find that they have legal responsibilities for their parents' care. For example, in a paper on the abandonment of older people – referred to by medical professionals as "granny dumping" – one legal scholar explains that in some states in the United States, children can be prosecuted for neglecting or abandoning a parent if they are considered by the state to be their parent's caregiver.[69] However, in a recent review on elder care in the United

States, the authors explain that, although 29 states have filial responsibility statutes, there is little uniformity in how these laws are interpreted or enforced. They conclude that: "Americans tend to value independence, individuality, and self-sufficiency, and adult children taking on the responsibility of caring for their parents is antithetical to the concept of individuality".[70]

Although I grew up with a particular model of how a family should be, what I have learnt is that there is no one way that parents and children support one another. I have also learnt that there is no one cultural understanding of what it means to be a "good" child, and that, similarly, there is no one answer to the question of to what extent children have legal duties for their parents' care. But while there is a great deal of variation in what we think it is that "good" daughters and sons do, I have also learnt that there are arguably few, if any, countries in which there are no expectations at all.

The age of responsibility

When they are young, what is it exactly that "good" sons and daughters should do? Should children help out with chores around the house, assisting their parents with tasks like laundry and cleaning? Should children anticipate that their parents will require help if they have had a long and difficult day at work? And at what age is it appropriate for children to be considerate of their parents' needs and participate in the running of their households?

In many families, children have substantial responsibilities from a young age. One kind of family in which this pattern can occur is that in which parents and their children have emigrated from one country to another. If the new country is one in which the parents' native language is not spoken, children can find themselves translating for their parents. This is not a small population, given that migration is far from a rare occurrence. As of 2020, the International Organization for Migration estimates that the number of international migrants is almost 272 million globally.[71]

Moving to a new country can be a time of enormous change, and a growing field of research explores the experiences of the children in these families who are known as child language brokers. One researcher who has spoken to adolescents about what it is like to translate for their parents is Dr Humera Iqbal at the Thomas Coram Institute at University College London. Dr Iqbal explained why it is that the children in these families often have more responsibilities than other children their age:

When families migrate, the language that is spoken in the new country may be different to their native language that they speak at home. This poses lots of challenges for settling in. However, children often pick up this new language faster than their parents, through attending school where they are surrounded by others speaking it. They inevitably start helping out their family in different ways. For example, if Mum has to go to the shops and she needs to ask for something a child might translate for them, or if Mum and Dad are watching TV together they might need a bit of a commentary on what's going on.

However, children who perform this role do more than simply translate words. Dr Iqbal told me that in translating for their parents, children can often be required to go into places in which children are typically absent, like banks and police stations, and can also become involved in important conversations that require sophisticated decision-making:

When you go to a new country there are so many things you have to do. You have to sort out where you're going to live, you have to set up a bank account and parents will need help with those tasks if they don't speak the language. Some children might even have to attend parents' evening and translate what their teacher said back to their parents. Children also have to make decisions on what to translate and those can be big decisions. Sometimes in order to avoid a conflict and protect their parents they might reword or choose not to translate things that people have said if they are racist and unkind.

What I have learnt in talking to Dr Iqbal is that in families that have migrated, children can find themselves taking on responsibilities that are more than linguistic: children can find themselves taking on a key role in how the family functions. And in many families, the fact that children take on these roles is in accordance with their cultural understanding of what a family is and what it is that family members should do for one another. Dr Iqbal explained:

> Thinking about what it is that these children do brings up the question of what is a "normal" childhood? What should children be doing? There is this idea in Europe and North America that childhood should be a time of play, being carefree, and that kids should be kids. But there are different ways of thinking about family. The idea that children should pitch in or have responsibilities is very common in other cultures.
>
> There is also often such a negative rhetoric around being a migrant. Some people might ask: Why are the parents not integrated? Why do they not learn English? Why are they depending on their kids? But it takes time to learn a new language as

an adult. Children are typically so much faster at picking up a new language.

As Dr Iqbal has alluded to, there is no one universal understanding of what it is that a "good" child does. And children who translate for their parents are not the only kinds of children who take on roles of responsibility in their families from a young age. Another type of family in which this happens are those in which parents have a mental or physical health problem or a disability. In these families, children often have to provide regular, significant care for their family members. Children who take on this role when they are under the age of 18 are often referred to as "young carers", and although the term might be unfamiliar, current data indicates that between 2 and 8 per cent of children in advanced industrialized capitalist societies are young carers.[72]

To understand more about the experiences of sons and daughters who care for their parents from a young age, I spoke with Dr Lynn Kettell at Edge Hill University, whose research has explored the experiences of children who provide care for a family member. I was curious to know what kind of roles and responsibilities the children in these families take on. Dr Kettell explained:

Caring for parents tends to involve hands-on physical care, although sometimes it's emotional support, particularly if it's a parent with mental health or addiction issues. The kind of task young carers do are things like cooking, cleaning, shopping and jobs around the house. But their responsibilities might also involve help with personal care, so washing and showering and physical care, helping a parent get in and out of bed or their wheelchair. Their roles might involve collecting medication or taking younger siblings to school and picking them up – it's quite a broad range of things really.

In addition to learning about the roles that the children in these families perform, I was curious to know why it is that this role tends to be an invisible one, rarely addressed in the media or shown in television or in film. Dr Kettell explained:

I feel like in some senses young carers are an invisible group. Some families prefer to "keep it in the family". And some young people don't recognize that what they actually do is caring and so it's not deliberately hidden, it's just because they don't realize that there's a name or a label for what they're doing. What I found in talking to young people is that there's quite a bit of stigma for some of them about admitting to others that their mum or dad has any kind of problem or issue that means that they require care. Some young carers don't want other people to know.

In learning about the experiences of children who translate for their parents and children who are "young carers", what I have learnt is that in many families, children have substantial duties that are integral to the functioning of their families. As for the question as to whether this is appropriate, there is no one easy answer. Perhaps in an ideal world, from a Western perspective at least, we might hope or expect that a parent would look to another appropriate adult to meet their needs for practical and emotional support. But parents and their children live in the real world, not an ideal one, and in many families, parents and children find that there are few alternative sources of support available to them.

What motivates children to care for their parents towards the end of their lives?

In older age, parents are more likely to experience poor health. They are therefore more likely to find themselves needing assistance with practical tasks such as household chores, travel to and from appointments, and the organization of their care. According to the narratives of the family story, dutiful daughters and loyal sons will gladly step up to fulfil this need. But do the daughters and sons who provide care for their parents in older age do so out of a sense of love, duty and a desire to reciprocate the care that they received as children? Or are their motivations a little more complicated than these simple storylines suggest?

The assumption that family members will support one another in times of need is not just one that runs throughout the narrative of the family story; rather, it plays a key role in how governments respond to the demands of population ageing. Around the world, the average number of children a woman gives birth to is declining and people are living longer than ever before: the number of people who are classified as being "older" is therefore rising. A report published by the UN in 2019 explains that there were 703 million people aged 65 or over in the world in 2019 and that the number of older people is projected to more than double to 1.5 billion by 2050.[73]

Therefore, the billion-dollar question is: How will governments cope with the costs of care for the rising number of older people who will require it? And the answer is: Families and friends – but mostly, families. For example, across 37 countries in the Organisation for Economic Co-operation and Development (OECD), studies have found that it is family and friends who are the most important source of care for people with long-term care needs.[74]

Informal care is far from evenly distributed. In a review of research on family relationships in later life, the authors explain: "Caregiving remains a gendered task, with wives and daughters providing the most care, although siblings, sons, husbands, and grandchildren also commonly care for aging relatives".[75] And when it comes to caring for a parent, daughters are more likely to provide care for their parents than sons. For example, the findings of one large-scale study in the United States confirmed that daughters, on average, provided twice as much care to their elderly parents than sons.[76] The author of this study went on to explain that although there is evidence to suggest that the gender gap is narrowing in some countries when it comes to housework and childcare, this shift does not appear to be happening when it comes to who provides care to parents.

There are many factors besides gender that influence a person's decision as to whether to be an informal carer. One such factor is their attitudes and beliefs about what it is that "good" children do. For example, one group of researchers looked at the findings of 46 studies that had explored the experiences of Chinese, Filipino, Japanese, Korean and Vietnamese caregivers living in the United States and

Canada. They found that the daughters and sons in these families had a strong sense of filial responsibility, and that they wanted to give back to their parents for the care that they had received from them as they were growing up.[77]

In addition to duty, the quality of the relationship between the parent and child is important. In a review of studies exploring people's decisions about caring for an older person, the authors explain that children who are most likely to care for a parent are those who have a positive relationship with them.[78] However, children do not only care for parents in the context of a positive relationship. In a recent review with the title "Caregiving for parents who harmed you", the authors explain that in the United States it is estimated that between 9 and 26 per cent of sons and daughters have experienced abuse and neglect by the parent for whom they provide care.[79] In reviewing 14 studies on childhood abuse and caregiving, the authors go on to explain that children often become carers for their parents because they feel that they have little or no choice in the matter due to limited finances or an inability to access formal systems of care.

Researchers have identified other factors that influence a child's decision as to whether to care for a parent, many of which are practical in nature. For example, one review identifies that geographical location matters: do they live close to the person who requires care?[78] And time matters too: do they have the capacity to perform a caring role given the other responsibilities that they have in life, such as being an employee or a parent? Other factors that influence people's decision-making include the amount of support that is available from family members, friends and the wider community.

The findings of these studies suggest that sons' and daughters' decisions as to whether to provide care for a parent do not come down to love and duty alone. This complexity was echoed in a recent blog piece that was published in the *Guardian* newspaper under the moniker of "the reluctant carer".[80] He describes his route to caring for his parents in the following way:

People react kindly when I tell them I look after my folks, but things are not as selfless as they seem. I care, but I am also captive. When I first came home, temporarily I imagined, to help them through a difficult patch, I had a house, a marriage and some semblance of a career. That was more than 12 months ago. Then the work project that had absorbed the previous two years and all my money came to nothing, my relationship collapsed, and there was a further decline in my parents' health. Which is more or less how I found myself back in a room and a town I left in the late 80s, caring for people in their late 80s. My siblings work and I am the best person for the job, in part since I have nowhere else to go.

While the narratives of the family story dictate that daughters and sons will care for parents out of love and duty, people's decisions as to whether to care for a parent in older age are a little more complicated. And the question of who cares for the ageing population is an incredibly important one. In a recent review, Family Policy Consultant Theodora Ooms explains that the question of who should provide care for the older people who need it is the "sleeping giant" of family policy. She explains that it is this question that is "poised to become the most important, complicated, and most visible issue that will and should dominate family policy for a long time to come".[81]

Can children abuse their parents?

Parents and children are expected to love one another and treat one another with respect. The fact that abuse occurs in this relationship is entirely absent from the narrative of the family story. But why is it that we rarely address the possibility that sons and daughters can abuse and neglect their parents? Is it because it rarely happens?

I was surprised to learn that the definition of elder abuse is broad. Elder abuse does not apply only to abuse of an older person by a son or a daughter, but refers to abuse that is perpetrated by anyone with whom the older person is in "a relationship of trust".

And I was surprised to find how common elder abuse is. In a review of research on elder abuse conducted in 28 countries, the authors concluded that the world prevalence rate of elder abuse was approximately 16 per cent, affecting 1 in 6 older adults worldwide.[82] And although most studies on elder abuse have been conducted in high-income countries, prevalence rates have been found to vary according to geography, with elder abuse being most common in Asia at 20 per cent, followed by Europe at 15 per cent and the Americas at 12 per cent.

I also learnt that there are different categories of elder abuse, with the most common being psychological or emotional, which includes name-calling, scaring, destroying property and restricting access to friends and family, which is estimated to affect 12 per cent of older people. This is followed by financial abuse, which refers to illegally misusing an older person's money, property or assets, which is estimated to affect 7 per cent of older people. Another kind of abuse includes neglect, referring to a failure to meet an older person's basic needs that include food, housing, clothing and medical care, affecting 4 per cent of older people. And finally physical abuse and sexual abuse are less common, affecting 3 per cent and 1 per cent of older people respectively.

While elder abuse can be committed by a range of people with whom the victim is in a relationship of trust, it is not unusual for the perpetrator to be a son or a daughter. One review concluded that in the United States, Israel, North America and Europe the most common perpetrator of elder emotional and physical abuse is a spouse or partner, whereas in Asian countries the most common perpetrators are children and children-in-law.[83] As with other kinds of abuse that occur within the family, most researchers believe that the abuse of a parent by a son or a daughter is under-reported. I spoke with researcher Dr Jennifer Storey at the University of Kent, who explained:

> There are several reasons that the reporting of elder abuse is low. The abusers of older people are often their children and people are extremely reluctant to get their children into trouble. Parents don't want to report their children and they don't want them going to prison, so this can lead to an underestimation

of prevalence. There is also a lot of shame around elder abuse – parents might think, I raised this person – and therefore feel shame or blame themselves. And then there's the fear held by some victims of not being believed or being placed in a care facility because they are saying these things. There is also fear around losing help, like losing the person who drives you to the doctor. With victims you see a lot of minimization and denial of the abuse, as well as what I call "excessive loyalty", which all reduce help seeking. What I mean by excessive loyalty is that most parents would do almost anything for their kids but there is a point at which we stop because it's detrimental to our health or our safety. Excessive loyalty is when the parent doesn't draw this line and puts themselves at risk of harm. There's a lot that parents will do for their kids, and rightfully so, but there should be a limit at the point that it becomes a danger to them.

Dr Storey's explanation stood out to me because I hadn't heard someone describe "excessive loyalty" as a problematic aspect of parenthood before, given that this is a quality that is so central to the way that we think "good" parents – especially "good" mothers – should be. As well as wanting to know why parents deny or minimize the fact that they have been abused by their child, I was interested to learn more about the sons and daughters who perpetuate abuse. This is a question that Dr Storey had recently addressed in a review of the literature, so I asked her to explain what she had found. She replied:

There are different assumptions about why people perpetrate elder abuse. One now generally outdated theory is the caregiver stress model, where the dynamic in the family is that the older person relies on their caretaker, and that their caretaker can find caregiving so difficult that they eventually snap and abuse the older person. I rarely see this dynamic in my research. There was also an assumption that elder abuse was based on a revenge model – you abused me and now I am abusing you to get revenge. Again, I have rarely seen this dynamic. More often what I see is a perpetrator with a series of life problems. Sometimes adult children are still living with their parents, and they are financially dependent on them, and have limited or poor relationships with others. That is the dynamic I see most often. And there are certain risk factors that make people more likely to engage in abuse. We know that perpetrators often have physical or mental health problems. Similarly, those who engage in substance abuse are more likely to abuse, and perpetrators tend to get stressed out more easily and they tend to have a lack of empathy, often having problems with relationships.".

In addition to learning about those sons and daughters who are more likely to perpetrate abuse, I wanted to know why it is that elder abuse is a topic that is rarely acknowledged or addressed. Dr Storey explained:

One reason may be ageism. Our society tends to value youth and devalue older people who are seen as less useful. This could perhaps then lead to less attention paid to issues relevant to older adults. Another reason is discomfort. When I tell people what I research they tend to get uncomfortable, and ask how I could focus on such a sad or upsetting issue. So, I think one reason that we don't talk about elder abuse is that this is something that we could have to face in the future and it scares us. We can do research on child abuse – we're not children anymore and we all want to protect children. But when we look into elder abuse, we must acknowledge that we will get older and more vulnerable, and we tend to fear this. Thus thinking about ageing and this added risk can be uncomfortable and perhaps that is one reason why this topic has received less attention.

Although I used to think of the abuse of older people as being rare – if I thought of it at all – I can now appreciate that children do abuse their parents and that this is more common that I would have expected. I have also come to understand that those who perpetrate abuse do so for a range of different reasons, and that it cannot be simply or always explained as an act of revenge by children who were abused by their parent in childhood. And like the other kinds of abuse between family members, I have learnt that elder abuse can be particularly shameful for victims. Parents have raised a child who is now abusing them, and to address this fact would mean getting their child in trouble. It is no wonder, then, that the abuse of parents by their children is a reality that is surrounded by secrecy, stigma and shame.

A role with few rules but great expectations

The role of parent is well defined: parents are expected to be responsible for their children's care, and these responsibilities are legally enforceable. And although it is a demanding role, being a parent is an identity that is praised, and the challenges of raising children are generally, if not always, acknowledged; few people who have been a parent, or have ever been around children, would dismiss it as being easy.

In contrast, being a good child is a role that lacks a clear, universal script. Being a child is also less of an aspirational role than that of parent, with loyal sons and daughters rarely receiving the praise reserved for hard-working mothers and dedicated dads. But while the role of child is a blurry one that is often unacknowledged, it would be wrong to think that it lacks substance. Because what I have learnt is that the responsibilities and duties of being a child can be substantial; being a "good" son or daughter can be a role that demands effort, dedication and sacrifice.

In many families, children care for their parents from a young age. They do this for different reasons and to different extents, but in many families, parents are reliant on their children to fulfil significant roles in their lives and in the functioning of their families. And in adulthood, many children take on the role of caring for a parent in older age. Although the narratives of the family story dictate that this is a labour of love, duty and sacrifice, there is no one reason why sons and daughters do so; some sons and daughters fulfil these roles out of duty or obligation, and some perform this role even when they have experienced neglect and abuse from their parent when they were growing up. Others might find that they perform this role because there are few alternatives available to them.

It is not uncommon for parents to experience abuse at the hands of their children. Just like child abuse, the high prevalence of elder abuse is entirely absent from the family story. But although it is deeply taboo, it is a common occurrence that it is essential to address. Because it is only when we address it that we can understand what it is, why it happens and how we can best support those who are victims of it.

six

How do sons and daughters feel?

There is no contradiction between loving someone and feeling burdened by that person; indeed, love tends to magnify the burden.

Andrew Solomon, *Far from the Tree: Parents, Children, and the Search for Identity*[43]

Whereas the last chapter focused on what it is that good children do, this chapter is focused on how it is that children feel. How do children feel when they have responsibilities for their parents from a young age? And how does it feel to care for a parent towards the end of their life? Are these roles in which sons and daughters feel pride and connection? Or are these roles in which children feel burdened, resentful or under-appreciated?

And then, in recognition that many children will not give care to a parent – and that many parents will not want to receive it even if it is offered – this chapter will explore children's feelings when they are not actively supporting their parents. It will explore how children feel when they encounter experiences that are missing from the narratives of the family story, when children do not feel that their parents' love for them is unconditional or lifelong. Specifically, this chapter will explore how it feels to be rejected by a parent, and how it feels to be estranged from a mother or a father in adulthood.

How does caring for a parent from a young age affect children's lives?

As we explored in chapter five, many children have substantial duties of care when it comes to the functioning of their families. So how do children feel when they have these roles? Do they feel burdened by them, longing for the freedom to pursue their own interests and put their own needs first? Or do they feel grateful to have the opportunity to contribute to their family? Perhaps their experiences evade the simple categorization of "good" or "bad".

Numerous studies have explored the experiences of children in families that have migrated from one country to another. As we explored in chapter five, when families have moved to a new country in which their native language isn't spoken, the children in these families can find themselves being a translator for their parents. In speaking with Dr Humera Iqbal, whose research explores the experiences of children who fulfil these roles in their families, I came to understand that there is no one way that being a translator for their parents influences children's lives. Dr Iqbal explained:

A lot of the children that I have worked with recognize that they have a sense of responsibility and they are also aware of the fact that their parents have given up so much to get them there.

They speak about the sacrifices that their parents have had to make in order to better their future, so they are happy to do this work if it helps their parents. But I also don't want to paint a picture that kids are always happy to take time out for interpreting and translation work for their families, because sometimes they find it gets in the way of them being teenagers – meeting friends, studying, working or just watching shows. It can also be physically and mentally tiring work, especially when they find themselves interpreting in the middle of an argument, or trying to interpret complex medical and legal terms.

Just as translating for parents can be experienced in both positive and negative ways, so too is caring for a parent with a physical disability or a mental health problem. In speaking with Dr Lynn Kettell at Edge Hill University, whose research explores the experiences of "young carers" who perform this role in their families, I came to appreciate that here, too, children's experiences are not necessarily wholly positive or negative, but rather a combination of the two. Dr Kettell explained:

I think that there can be a real sense of anxiety for young carers, particularly if they live in a single parent household and it is the parent who has the illness or disability, because what would happen to them if their parents needed to go into hospital, or worse? It can also be difficult for young people to balance their education with their caring responsibilities, so they might have difficulty concentrating in school because they are worried about what is happening at home. But what young people can often find the hardest is the fact that they can't socialize with their friends, or that their ability to go out with friends is limited. However, some of the positives of caring for a parent include being able to stay together as a family, because that might not happen otherwise. And young carers typically have a sense of love for their family member who needs support, and a real sense of purpose in being the one who helps them.

In providing care for a parent from a young age, children can experience both benefits and burdens. But although the children in these families might think of their roles in a positive light, this does not necessarily mean that these are roles without negative consequences. Psychologists often think of children's experiences through the lens of "parentification" or "parent–child role confusion". These are terms that are used to refer to patterns that can occur in family relationships when children perform roles that are usually carried out by parents or adults.

Parent–child role confusion can occur in many different families, not just those in which children translate for their parents or provide care for a parent with a disability or mental health problem. For example, in a recent review of research on this topic, the authors explain that parent–child role confusion can occur when parents who are arguing with one another look to their child to meet their need for emotional comfort, or when they expect their child to take on the role of referee and resolve their conflict.[84] It can also occur if a parent who is struggling to process a traumatic loss relies on their child for a sense of comfort. And in families in which parents experience alcoholism, depression and borderline personality disorder, parents can seem vulnerable and in need of help, which can result in their children stepping in to take control. In these scenarios, there is a role-reversal: rather than a parent caring for a child, a parent looks to their child to meet their needs.

Just as parent–child role confusion can emerge for different reasons, it can affect children's lives in different ways. For example, in the review of research on this topic that I have drawn on above, the authors explain that children can develop a set of guidelines in their heads that tells them that they are only worthy of love if they care for others. The authors go on to describe how, if a child feels responsible for how their parent feels or behaves, that child might suppress their own thoughts, feelings and desires, which can negatively impact on their lives and their relationships with other people. While the authors acknowledge that research in this field is growing and that many questions remain unanswered, they conclude: "It is clear that role-confusion may affect child development negatively but this is not widely recognized or addressed."

However, the outcomes of parent–child role confusion are not always or necessarily negative. For example, if children feel like their roles and duties in the family are fair, and that they are valued within their culture, these roles have been identified as ones that can contribute to increased feelings of self-worth and competence. And if they are roles that can be achieved – for example, completing a specific chore – they are more likely to be positive for children than those roles that are open-ended or impossible to achieve, such as trying to help a depressed parent feel better.

What I have learnt, then, is that caring for a parent from a young age can be a burden. Children can lose out on time with their friends, and they can feel worried about their parents, monitoring their moods and feeling responsible for the emotional climate of their homes. These experiences are not those that we might expect when we think of childhood as being a time of worry-free exploration and play.

However, children who care for their parents from a young age also describe loving their parents and wanting to help them, and researchers have identified that there can be benefits from caring for and supporting a parent from a young age, such as increased feelings of competence and empathy. Children's feelings about their roles will likely change as they grow older, but what really matters is that children's voices are heard and that their roles in their families are acknowledged.

Is caring for a parent at the end of their life a privilege or a burden?

Although it is not a universal experience, many sons and daughters care for a parent when they experience illness, frailty or disability in older age. And in doing so, sons and daughters will likely receive praise and admiration. But despite this admiration, few will think of caring for a parent in older age as being easy. Films about this experience tend to highlight the heartache, pain and burden of this experience. So for those daughters and sons who take on the role of caring for their parent, how does this experience impact their lives, and what is this experience like?

Perhaps unsurprisingly, studies find that being an informal carer – that is, caring for a family member or friend, typically without pay – can have a negative impact on people's health and well-being. In a comprehensive review of studies in this field, the authors describe how those who perform this role are more likely to experience mental health problems such as anxiety, stress and depression, as well as injuries like back pain. They also explain that the financial demands of caring can be a further source of stress and worry, particularly if carers have left paid employment or reduced their hours of work in order to provide care.[85]

Caring for a parent is also acknowledged to be a particularly challenging experience. Sons and daughters typically have to juggle their caring responsibilities alongside other roles, like being a partner, parent and employee. And the nature of caring can itself be difficult, with caring becoming harder over time as a parent's health declines. Yet despite its challenges, or perhaps to some extent because of them, caring for a parent can also be a meaningful experience that is greatly valued. In a review of 19 studies about the experiences of adult children caring for their ageing parents, the authors summarized, "All studies show that caregiving for ageing parents can be burdensome at times and satisfactory at other times".[86]

The quality of the relationship between a child and their parent also determines what this experience is like. For example, in a review of 55 studies that explored sons' and daughters' experiences of caring for a parent, the authors concluded that children experienced higher levels of burden when their relationship with their parent was characterized by disappointment and conflict.[87]

While studies identify that sons and daughters who care for their parents can often feel burdened, it can be hard to appreciate what this actually feels like. Many readers have been drawn to the writing of "the reluctant carer", mentioned in chapter five: a blogger who cares for his parents, whose pieces have featured in the *Guardian* newspaper and are due to be published in a book in 2022. I reached out to "the reluctant carer" to ask him what caring for his parents had been like. His answer was not a simple one, but it was an honest one. He explained:

I have learnt a lot about myself. I feel broadened by the experience and think it's been useful and good for me. But I have found caring for my parents to be very psychologically and physically difficult. You become like a hypervigilant parent, you're sensitive to any sound in case someone has fallen. Caring for a parent is also full of decisions and risk and uncertainty and all of these decisions are on you. You are suddenly given a load of drugs and a person and some vague instructions about what to do. It can feel consuming and demanding and there are times when it feels unfair. And then, there are moments when you think, have I done enough?

In caring for a parent, you can't help but ask yourself, What do you talk about when you talk about love? Because this isn't Valentine's Day. It isn't idyllic. Ambivalence comes to the fore. I still lose my patience with my mum and I feel terrible about it, but it can be so demanding. I love that woman but it's not straightforward. Because even if you'd had a good day, you end up just thinking, please die, painlessly, soon. Because the longer that this goes on for, the harder it gets. And you have to be able to allow yourself to have those thoughts.

In describing the reality of caring for his parents, "the reluctant carer" enabled me to understand that this experience is not one that can be tidily categorized as a burden or a blessing. I was curious to know what he thought it was that drew people to his work. He explained that the answer was in the messiness of his experience:

Stories are incredibly useful ways for us to frame things. But if anything, my story is about the danger of stories. I found the only way to care for a parent is to live in the moment. And the greatest freedom came when I let go of any expectations that I had. Because anytime I tried to create a story, the reality would shift. The reality became so chaotic, so unpredictable, so outside of reason or reckoning, that if I tried to view it as a story with a beginning, middle and an end, it would not conform. Especially when I was at my most fragile, vulnerable and stressed.

The story would not conform to what it is to be a mother, father, son, daughter or sibling. It would not conform to those ideas of being good, bad, dutiful, errant, angry, calm or loving. None of those things quite fit. So what I chose to do was convey the irregularity of it and the conflict of it. And when people have written to me to share their experiences with me, I can see that that is what has appealed to them.

As I have found to be the case for so many of the experiences that I have explored in relation to family, it seems that here, too, the plot-lines of the family story are inadequate, because there is no one experience and no one story of what it is like to be a son or daughter who cares for their parent when they are ill, frail or disabled. And I have also learnt that, for those who are in this role, letting go of any expectations or storylines as to how it should unfold can be a gift.

What happens when children do not feel accepted for who they are?

A common assumption about parenthood is that this is a love that is stronger and more enduring than any other kind of love. The love that parents have for their children is expected to be unconditional. But what happens when children feel like they are loved by their parents, but only if and when they meet certain conditions? And what if these conditions are not just about the things that they do, but about who they are?

One researcher who has studied how children experience rejection is Professor Rin Reczek at Ohio State University in the United States. In one in-depth study, Professor Reczek and their colleague Dr Emma Bosley-Smith explored the experiences of 76 adults who identified as LGBTQ.[88] They found that most – 85 per cent – had experienced rejection from their parents, which occurred in different ways. For example, some parents treated their child's identity as if it was a phase, whereas other parents failed to use their child's chosen pronouns to refer to their gender identity. Other parents had a "don't ask, don't tell" policy about a child's identity, avoiding any topic of conversation that was related to sexuality or gender, while a number of children in the study described how their parents threatened to stop supporting them practically, financially and emotionally if they did not conform to their expectations.

I spoke to Professor Reczek to ask them why it is that rejection is such a common experience for children who identify as LGBTQ. They explained:

Even though some countries might have these progressive laws, like same-sex marriage laws, parents and children live in a homophobic society in which we expect that people will be heterosexual and identify as being a man or a woman. And parents have expectations for their children, whether they want to admit it or not, and those expectations are typically that they are going to have grandchildren and that their children are going to live a "normal" life: that they will marry a person of a different sex and have children.

These expectations cause a lot of pain when they're not met and I can understand that it's painful because society values those life events. But parents need to work on that, because they need to accept their children for who they are. And if they can't then it really becomes a huge issue. Either their kid starts hiding who they are, they create distance in the relationship, or there's just intense conflict every time they see each other.

In the study that I've described on the previous page, almost all of the children who took part wanted to maintain an active relationship with their parents despite the fact that they experienced their parents as rejecting a key part of who they are. The researchers found that the children in the study maintained their relationships by using a number of strategies. One such strategy was that of education; children tried to educate their parents about their identity in the hope that their parents would become more accepting over time. Another strategy was that of keeping a low profile, hiding their identity to avoid conflict. Another approach that children used was to be open about who they are but to accept the fact that their parents were not going to accept them. And another strategy was the creation of boundaries, reducing contact with their parents in order to manage feelings of pain and strain, which was often the last stop before permanent estrangement.

In exploring these different strategies that children use to maintain their relationships with their parents, we can understand more about the nature of these relationships. Because although the narratives of the family story dictate that the love between parents and children is natural and instinctive, what the findings of studies like the one I have described above suggest is that family relationships are like those between any other human beings: they require work. Professor Reczek explained:

I think it's a disservice to frame the love and bonds between family members as a natural occurrence. Because when we do that, then the people who don't have love feel that something is wrong with them. Just like any other relationships, you need to acquire a skill set to cultivate good relationships. Because the relationships between family members need work. Just because you have shared history or biology or legal status, does not imply that you have similar interests or like each other.

And people feel a lot of pain when they either lose that tie or have a bad relationship, but they could actually feel much more free if they could let go of those expectations of what the family should be.

The lesson that there is freedom in letting go of expectations is one that has continued to arise as I have explored how it is that children feel about their relationships with their parents. And so too has the lesson that the relationships between children and their parents involve a broad range of experiences, not just those of love and connection.

In countries around the world, psychologists have studied the extent to which children feel accepted or rejected by their parents. A leading voice in this field is that of Professor Robert Rohner, Professor Emeritus of Family Studies and Anthropology at the University of Connecticut. In a review of his many decades' worth of research, Professor Rohner and his co-author Professor Lansford explain that accepting behaviours are those that are loving, nurturing and supportive.[89] These behaviours include praise, compliments, being available to talk to and showing interest in what a child does, and making a child feel loved, liked and important.

On the other side of the coin, rejecting behaviours include saying unkind things, hurting a child's feelings and paying little attention to them. Other examples of rejecting behaviours include making a child feel unloved if they misbehave, acting as if a child is a nuisance, being too busy to answer a child's questions and forgetting important things that children have said. Rather than people's experiences falling under the headings of "loved and accepted" or "unloved and rejected", Professor Rohner and Professor Lansford explain: "Individuals are neither accepted nor rejected in any categorical sense. Rather, they fall somewhere along a continuum".

Just as people's experiences of acceptance and rejection by a parent vary, so too does the level of support and love that they receive in their other significant relationships. But despite this variation, Professor Rohner and Professor Lansford explain that the studies in this field have identified certain patterns. For example, studies have found that those who experience significant rejection can experience intense, painful feelings of anger and resentment, which can lead them to close off emotionally from people in an effort to protect themselves from potential feelings of hurt. And, crucially, studies have found that it is not parents' perceptions of the relationships that matter, nor those of outside observers of the relationships, such as researchers. Rather, it is children's perceptions of whether they were accepted or rejected that go on to shape their feelings about themselves and the way that they engage in relationships with other people.

Although parents are assumed to be unconditionally loving, I have come to understand that children can feel rejected by a parent in many different ways. Some of the routes to feelings of rejection are obvious or blatant, like when a parent yells at a child, grabs them or hurts them. But there are less obvious ways that children can feel rejected by a parent too, such as when children feel like their needs or their wishes don't matter or when their parent withdraws their love by giving their child "the silent treatment". And these experiences are painful ones, with significant implications. Not only can rejection have a negative impact on children's relationships with their parents, sometimes severing them entirely, but they can have a negative impact on people's mental health and their feelings of worthiness. What I have learnt is that it is not enough that a parent says that they love their child: a child has to feel it.

How does being estranged from a parent affect children's lives?

Family members are assumed to love one another unconditionally. So what happens when children have little or no contact with their parents? Parents who are estranged from their children have been found to experience stigma, isolation and feelings of loss. Is estrangement experienced by children in a similar way? Or is this experience less impactful for children, whose identities and lives are less tied up with this relationship compared to their parents? When children and parents become estranged, are there "winners" and "losers"?

Children's experiences of estrangement vary in many important ways. One factor that it is particularly important to consider is how old children are when their relationships with their parents become strained and begin to deteriorate – because when children's relationships with their parents begin to break down in childhood and adolescence, estrangement can result in homelessness. This is not a rare occurrence. In a recent analysis of 49 studies that were conducted in 24 countries, the authors indicated that family conflict had been the route to homelessness for 32 per cent of youth who were homeless.[90] Homelessness is also more likely to be experienced by some children than others, with one review finding that, for people aged 12–25, identifying as LGBTQ was a key risk factor for becoming homeless.[91]

Although the relationships between parents and children can break down when children are young, most studies on estrangement have explored the experiences of adults. These studies have found that sons and daughters experience a range of emotions towards their estranged parents, including anger and hurt, but also empathy for their parents. For example, in an in-depth study conducted in Australia, Dr Kylie Agllias explored the experiences of 26 sons and daughters who were estranged from a parent. While some of the children in the study were aware that their parents had experienced a range of adversities in their lives, such as mental health problems, substance abuse issues, painful divorces and difficult childhoods, they also felt that these events did not excuse their parents' behaviour towards them or lessen their parents' responsibility for their actions.[92]

In addition to these powerful and sometimes mixed feelings, children often experience isolation, tending not to share the details of their estrangement with other people out of the fear that they will be judged. In one study conducted in the United States, 52 sons and daughters had intentionally created distance from a parent due to a negative relationship: the author of the study, Professor Kristina Scharp, concluded that "more often than not, adult children were, at best, met with confusion and, at worst, met with unwanted attempts at reconnection".[93] It is no wonder that children keep this aspect of their lives to themselves; when they do share the details of their estrangement with other people, they are rarely met with compassion and understanding.

As well as experiencing stigma about being estranged, children who have a distant relationship with a parent experience loss, even when they themselves have chosen to initiate the estrangement. For example, in the Australian study of adult children who initiated or maintained estrangement from a parent, sons and daughters described missing being a part of a family and the benefits that being a part of a family can bring, even if they did not miss the relationship that they had had with their estranged parent.[94]

When the relationships between parents and children break down in adulthood, estrangement appears to impact parents' and children's lives in similar ways, resulting in feelings of pain, experiences of isolation and loss. However, there is also one way that children's experiences of estrangement might differ from those of parents. For children, it appears that there can be positive outcomes that result from this experience as well as the more negative ones. To learn more about the more beneficial outcomes of estrangement, I spoke with Professor Kristina Scharp, who has many years of experience in speaking to sons and daughters who are estranged from their parents. She explained:

Estrangement can be a healthy solution to an unhealthy environment. So although it's difficult to distance yourself from a family member, it's also positive to leave any kind of abusive relationship, because the reasons for estrangement can be so severe. People don't become estranged because they got grounded once. Sometimes when there's arguments in a relationship, those are things that people can overcome. That's life, that's part of being in a relationship. But given the severity of the events and occurrences that can be the catalyst for estrangement, it can be positive for the people initiating that distance, because there was a pretty strong reason why they wanted to initiate that distance. Estrangement can be an ambivalent experience, with some things in life being harder but some things getting better. But at the point where you have what I call continuous estrangement, you've decided that the benefits of not being in that relationship outweigh the costs. And those costs were high.

Research on estrangement is small yet growing. Studies have mostly explored the experiences of those who have intentionally chosen to initiate distance from a parent due to a negative relationship; we therefore know little about those for whom it was their parent who initiated the estrangement, or those for whom determining the initiation of estrangement is less clear cut. We also know mostly about the experiences of daughters, and those who live in the UK, USA and Australia. With these limitations in mind, what I have learnt is that although there might be positive outcomes of estrangement from a parent, like feelings of safety, sons and daughters in this position also experience stigma and feelings of isolation and loss. And when these relationships break down when children are young, children can also experience the profoundly negative mental and physical health outcomes that accompany homelessness. Although it might be tempting to think of estrangement as a simple experience in which those who choose to initiate estrangement are the "winners" and those who do not wish to be estranged are the "losers", the reality appears to be more complicated. Because although there can be some positive outcomes for children who are estranged from a parent, children who are in this position experience both substantial and significant losses.

A vital perspective

Each of the lessons that I have learnt about children's feelings towards their parents reaches a similar conclusion: that there is no one simple story of what it means to be a child that can be categorized as "good" or "bad". When it comes to how children feel about their relationships with their parents, children experience a deep and diverse range of feelings, ranging from gratitude and acceptance to anger, shame and resentment.

When children are young and when they are grown, those who care for their parents will likely be praised as being particularly "good". And caring for a parent can be a deeply meaningful role, in which sons and daughters value the opportunity to give back to their parents. However, caring for a parent can also be a heavy role that is full of challenges and strain. And this seems to be especially true for those sons or daughters who care for a parent in the context of a challenging or abusive relationship.

The relationships that children have with their parents can also be complex when they do not have a caring role in the family. Although it is missing from the family story, many children experience rejection by their parents, which can be especially difficult when parents do not accept their children for who they are. I have come to understand that rejection does not necessarily occur only when a parent threatens to cut off financial support to a child. Rather, it can look like avoiding certain topics of conversation, or failing to take an interest in a child's life, feelings and experiences. Children can feel rejected for all sorts of reasons, in all sorts of ways.

What these lessons have taught me is that there is a fragility to the love between family members. Parents might say that they love their children, but this does not mean that their children will feel loved. And although children's feelings are often overlooked and undervalued, decades' worth of research conducted in countries all over the world has reached the same conclusion: whether children feel accepted or rejected by their parents matters. The child's perspective is a vital one; there is much to gain from listening, acknowledging and validating their experiences, and much to lose if we don't.

In the family story, the love between family members is unconditional. We assume that sons and daughters feel close to their parents and grateful for their investment in their lives. The family story is therefore one that obscures, rather than reveals, the reality of how sons and daughters feel towards their parents. Because, as with the other roles and relationships in the family, the reality is a little more complex, varied and less idyllic. In accepting and appreciating this complexity, we might be less likely to judge ourselves and other people who do not fall into the expected narratives of the family story.

seven

Growing up together: sibling relationships in childhood

People often describe their closest friends as being "like a brother", or "like a sister", to denote that theirs is a relationship that is particularly significant, deep and long-lasting. But the sibling relationship can also be a volatile one: when brothers and sisters are growing up together, laughter can turn to tears in the blink of an eye, with some studies finding that siblings fight as often as every 10 minutes.[95]

So what does a "normal" relationship between brothers and sisters typically look like in childhood? The first question this chapter will address is about sibling fighting. To what extent is shouting, pushing or hitting in the sibling relationship harmless or harmful? It will then explore the extent to which brothers and sisters have responsibilities towards one another. Are sibling relationships those between equals? Or do siblings have more substantial duties towards one another?

It will then ask why it is that sibling relationships turn out the way that they do. Are parents to blame if the sibling relationship is one of aggression, and are they to be congratulated if the sibling relationship is warm and close? And finally, this chapter will consider favouritism. Parents are expected to love their children equally and treat them in the same way, so what happens when siblings feel that their brother or sister is the star of the show? Is this a common experience that has little impact on their lives and relationships? Or are the feelings that accompany favouritism, like jealousy and feelings of unworthiness, ones that linger?

How much fighting between siblings is normal?

I grew up thinking that fighting with a brother or a sister was to be expected. I didn't think that behaviours like hitting, shoving and name-calling would be a particular cause for concern. And it turns out that I am not alone in this assumption. When it comes to the more violent interactions between siblings, Professor John Caffaro, an expert on sibling relationships, put it this way: "Parents often ignore it as long as nobody is killed; researchers rarely study it; and many psychotherapists consider its milder forms a normal part of growing up".[96] So to what extent is sibling fighting a problem? Is this something that parents should be deeply concerned about? Or is it simply a "normal" feature of the relationship between brothers and sisters?

Conflict between siblings is inevitable. Brothers and sisters who grow up together typically share toys and have to negotiate boundaries with one another. And rather than being thought of as harmful, psychologists acknowledge that it can present children with opportunities to develop various abilities, like understanding other people's thoughts and feelings, as well as presenting them with opportunities to hone their skills of negotiation and finding solutions to problems. However, on the other side of the coin, sibling relationships can be those in which children learn to be aggressive.

So how do we know when sibling fighting crosses the line from harmless into harmful? In a review of research on sibling bullying, the authors make a distinction between rivalry and bullying.[97] Whereas rivalry refers to infrequent or singular acts of aggression, bullying involves intentional and persistent aggressive behaviours and an imbalance of power. The authors stress that aggression isn't only physical, involving hitting, kicking or pushing, but can be verbal too, including name-calling, threats, excluding a sibling or spreading rumours about them.

Although this distinction between rivalry and bullying might seem simple, other researchers have used different terms to describe the more negative and potentially destructive interactions between siblings. For example, in one review, researchers argue that it is important to distinguish bullying from abuse, which they define as: "consistent but unpredictable physical or psychological torment involving brutal physical force or emotional devastation" (98). They go on to clarify that the defining features of sibling abuse are that it is unpredictable; that a sibling is unable to protect themselves from it; that there is a power differential between siblings; and that one sibling has an intent to harm, control or humiliate the other.

Unfortunately, the prevalence of sibling abuse is unknown, largely because this aspect of the sibling relationship is under-studied and researchers have used different terms to study it. However, those who study sibling relationships are in agreement about one thing: aggression in this relationship is common. In a review of research on sibling bullying that looked at studies conducted over the past 25 years, the authors found that 40 per cent of children are targets of intentional and persistent aggression every week, leading them to conclude that: "relationships with siblings are probably the most aggressive relationships that the majority of children will ever encounter during their childhood".[97]

Sibling bullying is most often reported in the relationships between brothers, or between older brothers and younger sisters. And it is most likely to occur in families in which parents are violent with their children or in which parents tend to have a "hands-off" approach to supervising their children's activities and behaviour with one another. Sibling bullying has also been found to be unique, because unlike bullying that happens between peers in the playground, brothers and sisters do not always fit tidily into the roles of "victim" and "aggressor". Rather, siblings most often fall into the category of "bully-victims", being both the victim of their sibling's aggression and also bullying their sibling in return.

Given that sibling bullying is so common, how seriously should we take it? It turns out that the consequences of sibling bullying are serious. The authors who reviewed 25 years of research on this topic concluded that persistent and intentional sibling aggression is associated with elevated levels of emotional distress, as well as diagnoses of depression and an increased risk of self-harm in early adulthood. A number of studies have also found that sibling bullying is related to bullying at school. For example, in a UK study of approximately 4,000 adolescents, researchers found that those children who were bullied by siblings were more likely to be bullied by their peers.[99] In a similar vein, those who were aggressive to their sibling were more likely to bully others at school or to be a victim of bullying.

But in determining the extent to which aggression and bullying are harmful, it is also important to think about the other qualities of the sibling relationship. For example, one group of researchers looked at a broad range of studies of sibling relationships in childhood and adolescence and concluded that sibling aggression is most concerning in those relationships in which there is a lack of warmth. They found that the warmer the relationship between siblings, the lower the risk of a child developing psychological problems in the context of sibling aggression.[100]

With these lessons in mind, I now think about sibling fighting in a different way. I no longer automatically assume that fighting is harmless but, instead, can appreciate that a number of different factors are important to consider, such as the severity and the frequency of the aggression, the sibling's intentions and the extent to which there is warmth alongside conflict in the relationship. Given this complexity, it seems that there is no one black and white answer as to whether fighting between siblings is good or bad. But one thing is for certain: although sibling relationships are assumed to be characterized by closeness, aggression is a common feature of these relationships.

What kinds of responsibilities do brothers and sisters have to one another?

Growing up, I expected that the older children in a family would be treated as being more mature and capable than their younger siblings. It therefore seemed logical that a parent might occasionally ask their eldest child to babysit or to "keep an eye" on their younger sibling. But that is about as far as I would have expected a sibling's duty to their brother or sister to go, as I generally thought of the sibling relationship as being one of equality.

In countries around the world, researchers have studied sibling caregiving, which refers to acts that children perform in caring for a brother or sister. Caring for a sibling can range from teaching or training a sibling to acquire new skills, to providing them with emotional support, such as comfort, companionship and advice, to the complete and independent full-time care of a sibling. In a review of research on sibling caregiving, the authors explain that in a number of non-Western cultures and in immigrant families living in the West, older children are often expected to care for their younger siblings in an involved, substantial way. For example, in immigrant Latino families in the United States, older siblings have been found to be involved in feeding and clothing their younger siblings in the morning, picking them up after school, supervising homework and modelling positive school behaviour.[101]

The responsibilities that siblings have to one another also differ according to the physical and mental health needs of the children in the family. And this is not a small population. One systematic review recently estimated that approximately 7–17 per cent of children have a sibling with a chronic physical illness or a mental health condition.[102] In one TED talk, Jamie Guterman describes her experience of growing up as the sibling of a child with special needs. In doing so, she describes how the siblings of children with special needs are sometimes referred to as "glass children". She goes on to explain that this term refers to the fact that: "people and family members often see straight through them to their sibling who has disabilities".[103]

Given the challenges that the siblings in these families can face, the charity Sibs was founded in the UK in 2001 by a group of individuals who had a sibling with a disability. The charity offers support to siblings in different ways, such as running support groups and developing a school-based intervention for the siblings of children with disabilities. I spoke with the CEO of Sibs, Clare Kassa, who explained that for those who grow up as a sibling of a child with a disability or chronic condition, the issue of responsibility is one that can weigh heavily. Clare told me that in some families, the expectation that a child will care for their sibling is assumed from a young age:

We know that children as young as seven are growing up thinking, I'm always going to have to look after my brother or sister. That's part of their identity, part of who they are as a sibling. Some won't of course but the majority will consider their brother or sister in their life choices. Some people choose not to get married because of their brother or sister, or not to have children, especially if there's a genetic implication in their families, and some won't move away or go to university.

Expectations as to who will care for a sibling can be particularly challenging in families in which parents don't talk to their children about the assumptions that they have about the future. This is something that Clare experienced in her own life, and it is a pattern that she observes in the families with whom she works. She explained:

In my family it was assumed that I would always look after my brother. And as my mum died when I was 18, that obviously came up quicker than I thought it might. I was one of four, but it was always assumed that I would look after my brother because I'm the youngest. And my parents didn't have that conversation with me. There are lots of unsaid things within families. There are also a lot of assumptions within families that once Mum or Dad can't do that anymore that a sibling will take it on. I met a parent recently who said, "I've always said to him, you two are always going to live together, you'll be in a flat together." At 10 years old this parent had written off the sibling's life choices, and it sometimes is like a joke within a family, or a bit of banter, which is how some parents see it. But actually, for that child it probably doesn't feel like banter.

It probably feels like it's pretty serious stuff, like your future is signed and sealed by the time you're 10.

Clare explained that the charity, Sibs, encourages parents and children to talk to one another and to have difficult conversations about the future. She also emphasizes that there is no one right choice or path for the siblings in these families because there is no one way that a sibling relationship is shaped by disability:

What we encourage as a charity is that people have conversations, have a family meeting, talk about it, get it out in the open – because I think there can be difficulties in families where that doesn't happen. It's important to talk to young siblings about their future needs. And this can be difficult for parents, because I think it can be terrifying for parents to think about the future. But those conversations need to happen.

And it's really important for siblings to know that they have a choice. That you don't have to do it, actually, you don't have to look after your brother or sister. You have a choice about what you do with your life. We support siblings to play whatever role they choose to play in their sibling's life, which might be full-on caring, or caring from a distance. It might be I want to be part of this, or I don't want anything to do with my brother or sister. We see all of that, all of those combinations, and sometimes these things change, and we're here to support people as these things change over the course of someone's life.

In speaking to Clare, I came to appreciate that in some families, a sibling might be expected to provide a level of care to their brother or sister that is both intense and enduring, and that this assumption is one that can shape children's lives from a young age. Rather than thinking of the sibling relationship as simply being one of equals, I can now appreciate that the kind of emotional or practical support that brothers and sisters provide to one another varies.

To what extent do parents shape sibling relationships?

It is tempting to think that parents are responsible for everything to do with children's lives, including the quality of the relationships between brothers and sisters. Some psychologists have put it this way: "In most families, sibling ties begin in childhood with parents writing the script".[104] When parenthood is viewed through this lens, mothers and fathers do not just have the responsibility of meeting the needs of each of their children as individuals, but they also have the responsibility of shaping the quality of their children's relationships with one another.

Parents play an important role in shaping the quality of their children's relationships with one another in direct ways that seem fairly obvious, as well as in indirect ways which are less obvious. One direct way in which mothers and fathers shape the sibling relationship is how they respond to their children's arguments with one another. Knowing exactly how and when to intervene in sibling conflict can be a challenging experience for parents, especially given that this can be such a frequent occurrence. To understand how parents handle their children's fights with one another, I spoke to Professor Claire Hughes, an expert in sibling relationships who is the Deputy Director of the Centre for Family Research at the University of Cambridge. Professor Hughes explained:

Once there are two children and they start squabbling, parents might resist getting involved, or they might step in to discipline a child. Others might intervene by helping their children to understand one another's different points of view and by encouraging them to start thinking about right or wrong – and it is these sorts of conversations where the arrival of a new sibling can really accelerate children's moral development, social development and emotional understanding.

As Professor Hughes suggests, when children are fighting, parents can encourage their children to understand one another's point of view while encouraging them to find their own solutions. This approach is referred to as mediation. A recent review found that parenting interventions that involved mediation training can have a positive impact on the quality of the sibling relationship.[105] In addition to acting as a mediator when their children fight, parents can also shape sibling relationships before their brother or sister is born. Professor Hughes explained how parents today often have more resources available to them to help them in this task compared to parents in the past:

I think there is often an assumption in psychology, and amongst people more generally too, that when a second child arrives, the eldest is going to be jealous and that they might find this really difficult. I know that in my own family I have my grandmother's baby book for my father and he had twin sisters when he was two. This book religiously documents all kinds of trivial

175

information and then at two it just says that my father is going on holiday. And I know why he's going on holiday – so that she can give birth to the twins, but there is no mention in the book about how he feels about the arrival of his siblings.

But now there are all sorts of lovely picture books to help prepare children as they become a brother or sister – "What's growing in mummy's tummy" – those sorts of things. And with that little bit of support, I think that for the large majority of families, the birth of a sibling is now much less difficult for children than it might have been compared to children in the past.

Parents therefore have a direct impact on sibling relationships, especially when it comes to preparing their child for the arrival of a brother or sister in the family. But in addition to this direct influence, parents also influence their children's relationships with one another in more subtle, indirect ways. In their book on sibling relationships, *Why Siblings Matter: The Role of Brother and Sister Relationships in Development and Well-Being*, Professor Claire Hughes and Dr Naomi White explain that numerous studies find evidence that behaviour and emotion in one relationship can spill over into another.[106] For example, one research team in the UK set out to explore the extent to which parents, and mothers in particular, shape the quality of the sibling relationship. Using data from a nationally representative sample of families in the UK, the researchers analyzed data from 118 families in depth.[107] They measured the quality of the sibling relationship, mothers' levels of anxiety and depression and mothers' engagement in positive and negative parenting. They found that the lower the levels of mothers' depression and anxiety, and the higher their engagement in positive parenting, and the more positive the relationship between siblings. These findings indicate that the mother's well-being and the quality of the parent–child relationship spill over into the sibling relationship. The authors explain that this could be a result of emotion contagion – simply put, that mothers pass on their mood to their children. Or another explanation is that of modelling: that the way that a mother responds to conflict sets an example for their children to follow.

But in addition to a spill-over effect, there is evidence of what researchers have called a "compensation effect": that if a relationship between a parent and one child is particularly negative, a child can turn to their sibling for comfort and to find solace. The ways that family relationships affect one another are complex rather than straightforward, but essentially, the takeaway message is this: psychologists rarely think of the relationships in the family unit as being separate, but rather they appreciate and explore the ways in which the different relationships in the family affect one another in both direct and obvious ways, as well as ways that are more indirect and subtle.

However, in focusing on parents alone, we are missing an important part of the sibling story. Because while parents are important, siblings exert an influence on one another independently of their parents, typically spending a great deal of time with one another outside of the direct supervision of parents or other adults. Perhaps it is unsurprising, then, that the quality of the sibling relationship is related to children's psychological well-being. For example, one group of researchers analyzed the findings of 34 studies, including data from 12,500 children and adolescents; they found that those whose sibling relationships were high in warmth and low in conflict had the best outcomes in terms of their mental health.[108]

And the way in which siblings influence one another becomes particularly clear in studies that explore adolescents' engagement in risky or antisocial behaviour. In a review of research on siblings, Professor Susan McHale at Penn State University and her colleagues explain that in adolescence, siblings influence one another in different ways. They can collude to undermine their parents' authority; they can become role models of deviant behaviour to one another, egging each other on to try new and dangerous behaviours; and they can act as gatekeepers to risky activities, like underage drinking and substance abuse.[109] One group of researchers analyzed the findings of 55 studies that had examined the risk factors that lead to children engaging in offending behaviours from childhood into adulthood. They concluded that siblings may be more influential in the development of offending behaviour than mothers.[110]

Given her vast experience in researching sibling relationships, I asked Professor Hughes to what extent she thought the responsibility for the sibling relationship lies in the hands of their parents, to which she gave the following thoughtful reply:

There is certainly robust evidence that suggests that parents influence the quality of their children's relationships with one another. But siblings affect one another's development in their own right too. The psychologist Professor Daniel Shaw has compared parents to being like doctors and siblings to nurses, which I think is apt. The doctors tend to get all the credit or the blame for an outcome, but actually it's the nurses who are there who are making a real difference. So although siblings are often overlooked, I think that they are a really important part of family life and child development.

What I have learnt is that when it comes to relationships between brothers and sisters, parents *are* writing the script, and that some parents today have a greater ability to access support in writing this script than parents did in the past, like being able to buy a children's book that will help prepare their child for the arrival of a sibling in the family. However, I can also now appreciate that while parents' actions and behaviours matter, they are not *all* that matters, because brothers and sisters influence one another's lives independently of their parents. I can appreciate that as they grow older, the children in the family are in the writing room too, actively contributing to the development of storylines, character arcs and plot twists.

What happens when there is a favourite child?

I grew up thinking that a parent's love for their child is unconditional and therefore perfect. And if a parent's love for their children is perfect, it must also be equal: a parent should love their children the same amount. But in real life, I know few people who would put their hand on their heart and say that this was what they had personally experienced as they were growing up. As clinical psychologist Dr Joshua Coleman shared in his book, *Rules of Estrangement: Why Adult Children Cut Ties and How to Heal the Conflict*: "Parents often tell their children 'We love you all the same,' but most children know that it's a lie. I knew that my mother favored me over my older brother. I was the baby for a full eight years and occupied that niche with all of the charm, innocence, and radiance that my conniving little heart could muster".[19] But to what extent is favouritism a problem? Is it a common experience that has little impact on children's lives and their family relationships, or is it something that can leave long-lasting wounds?

Those who study sibling relationships acknowledge that parents often treat their children differently, and typically accept that this is both understandable and unavoidable. In their book *Adult Sibling Relationships*, social workers Professor Geoffrey Greif and Professor Michael Woolley explain that children arrive at different times in their parents' lives.[111] For example, an older child might be born at a time when money is tight, and when there is little support available from family members and friends. However, their younger sibling might be born at a time when money is free-flowing, and when family members or friends are more able to offer practical, financial and emotional support. In some ways, siblings are born into different families, leading them to conclude: "Parents simply cannot raise their children in exactly the same way, no matter how much they love them and no matter how hard they try."

Psychologists also stress that treating a son and daughter differently is not necessarily bad, wrong or insensitive. I spoke with clinical psychologist and sibling researcher Dr Naomi White, who has studied the ways in which parental differential treatment affects children's well-being and the quality of sibling relationships. Dr White explained:

I think in Western cultures there is an emphasis on treating children the same. But I think to some extent parental differential treatment is unavoidable and to some extent it is good parenting. For example, if a parent has a child who is highly anxious and a child who is not anxious at all, they would probably treat them quite differently. And that's probably a good thing because the two children may respond better to two different parenting approaches. So I think we have to be careful that we don't always view differential treatment as universally bad.

So how does a parent's differential treatment affect children's lives? At first glance, the findings of studies on favouritism seem to be confusing. Because even though psychologists acknowledge and explain that parents who treat their children differently are not necessarily doing anything wrong – in fact, the differential treatment of children can be an indication that they are parenting their children sensitively – the outcomes of favouritism are generally negative. For example, in a review of studies on sibling relationships, the authors explain that the differential treatment of children by their parents is typically associated with a range of negative outcomes for children, such as lower levels of psychological adjustment and less positive sibling relationships.[109]

One research group explained this pattern in the following way:[108] As brothers and sisters typically spend time together, they will inevitably compare themselves to their sibling. If a parent is more loving to a brother or a sister, a child might think that this is reflective of a fault or lack in their own character, negatively impacting their self-esteem, which can lead to feelings of insecurity, anxiety and a sense of unfairness. This is not only the case for the sibling who feels that they are not the favourite, but for the sibling who is favoured too, who might feel guilty about the way that their parents treat them, while also fearing the loss of being in the top spot.

Therefore, in thinking about parental favouritism, it is not enough to only focus on what it is that parents do; an important piece of the puzzle is how children think and feel about the way that their parents treat them. And researchers have found that it is when children perceive their parents' differential treatment to be unfair that it can be particularly damaging. For example, in one study, 135 children and their older siblings were interviewed separately about their parents' distribution of affection and the way that they engaged in discipline. Children were found to have better mental health and self-esteem when they perceived that their parents' treatment of them was fair.[112]

Given Dr White's experience in studying sibling relationships, I asked her why it is that children's perspectives are so important when it comes to differential treatment. She explained:

In the research we can see that in families with a child with a disability, differential treatment isn't always related to bad outcomes for children and it's probably because it's more obvious why the child is treated differently. So I think it's really children's perception of that treatment that is important and whether they perceive it to be fair or unfair.

Children's perspectives also matter because children may be more aware of differential treatment than their parents, because children are often very sensitive to any differences in how they are treated by their parents. For example, in one of our studies a child brought up in an interview that they were really annoyed that their younger brother was staying up to the same time as them in the holiday. They thought that this was unfair because they didn't get to stay up that late when they were their younger sibling's age. The parent had no idea that this was even an issue. I think it's one of those things that if your sibling has a bigger piece of cake than yours, you're probably going to notice that!

And I also think that siblings aren't always on the same page – the way that parents treat their children can be perceived quite differently. And there could be lots of reasons for that. Siblings are often different ages, so they might have different perceptions of what is going on or different understandings of what is happening. And children might be less aware of differential treatment if they're the favoured one, whereas if you perceive that you are being treated worse than your sibling it's probably going to be more salient to you.

Although there is an assumption that a parent's love for their children is perfect and should therefore be equal, for many different reasons, this is not always achieved in reality. And I have also come to understand that even though it appears to be both commonplace and unavoidable, the differential treatment of children can have a negative impact on children's well-being and the quality of the sibling relationship. But what seems to really matter when it comes to favouritism isn't parents' behaviour in and of itself, but rather how the children in the family think and feel about the way that their parents treat them. Because the differential treatment of children that causes the greatest amount of damage is that which children perceive as being unfair.

One relationship, many roles

In delving into the research on siblings, I have questioned why it is that I have thought of certain kinds of behaviours – specifically, aggressive behaviours – as being "normal". In the family story – the way that we think families should be – there is no mention of aggression or deep and lasting hurt. Any kind of negativity is swept under the carpet, or it is minimized and turned into an amusing anecdote. But what I have learnt is that, for many children, aggression is a common experience and that just because it is common that does not mean that it is harmless. Although it is rarely spoken about, and although it happens in plain sight, sibling bullying has a long-lasting negative impact on people's lives and well-being.

In learning these lessons about brothers and sisters, I feel far less confident in my ability to make assumptions about how a "normal" sibling relationship functions and how it should feel. While I can now appreciate that sibling relationships are experienced in different ways – that some are characterized by a mix of warmth and conflict while others are dominated by aggression – I have also learnt that sibling relationships function in different ways too. In some cultures, taking a younger brother or sister to school, helping them with their homework and giving them meals from a young age might simply be thought of as being a good sibling. And in other families, taking on responsibilities towards a sibling with a disability might kick into gear in adulthood, when their parents can no longer fulfil this role. Just as aggression, pain and rejection are absent from the family story, so too are plotlines about the substantial obligations and duties that siblings can have to one another.

I have also come to understand that although we often think of parents as being responsible for every aspect of their child's life, including the quality of their relationship with their sibling, the reality is a little more complex. Parents certainly matter, and they play an important role in shaping this relationship. But I was surprised to learn that this influence can often be indirect, with parents "setting the tone" of their households. And I have learnt that there is a limit to parents' responsibilities too, as parents do not have total control over the sibling relationship: siblings influence one another's lives independently of their parents. In this way, children are not passive actors in the family play, but rather they are actively contributing to and creating their relationships with one another, in ways that can be constructive as well as destructive.

And when it comes to favouritism, I have come to understand that it isn't just what parents do or say that matters: the way that children think and feel about how their parents treat them is important. This has been a common theme in the chapters of this book. If we want to understand family relationships, we need to take children's perspectives seriously, because how a child thinks and feels about a family relationship matters.

eight

How do sibling relationships survive in adulthood?

Whenever families gather, siblings notoriously take up their accustomed positions and reproduce their original dynamics, as though the roles were etched on their brains, ready to be magically reconstituted when the cast reassembles.

J. Safer, Cain's Legacy: Liberating Siblings
From a Lifetime of Rage, Shame, Secrecy, and Regret[113]

In almost every book and academic paper, sibling relationships are described as being the longest relationships of our lives. This is an assumption that no doubt motivates parents to expand their families; in having two or more children, many will hope that their children will have someone in their life who they will know from childhood to adolescence, adulthood, older age and death.

But is this description an accurate one, or an assumption? In this chapter we will explore how brothers and sisters get along with one another in adulthood. It will ask questions like, How much contact is "normal" when it comes to siblings? And are some sibling relationships – like those between twins – different or special in any way?

This chapter will then explore how common events in family life, like the illness of a parent, can strain these relationships. And finally, this chapter will explore why it is that some relationships between brothers and sisters break down entirely.

What does a "normal" sibling relationship look like?

I have grown up with the idea that the bond between brothers and sisters is typically one of warmth and closeness. That at best, these relationships are like a lifelong friendship and a source of support through life's ups-and-downs. And perhaps at worst, I expected that brothers and sisters would speak over the phone or meet face-to-face a few times a year. Even if these relationships are distant for long stretches of time, it is often assumed that they will function as a safety net in times of need: that it is a relationship that people can pick up where they left off. But to what extent do these assumptions reflect the reality of sibling relationships?

The level of contact that siblings have with one another in adulthood varies. For example, in a sample of approximately 4,000 adults in the Netherlands, around half, 47 per cent, had face-to-face or phone contact at least once a month. However, the other half were in contact with one another less frequently: in the past year, 40 per cent had had contact a few times and 13 per cent had had contact no more than once.[114]

The findings of this study led me to wonder what kind of siblings see one another most often. And unsurprisingly, as with everything to do with family relationships, I found that gender plays an important role in how close and connected siblings are to one another over the course of their lives. The authors of a recent review on sibling relationships in adulthood confirmed that sister–sister pairs have the closest relationships across the lifespan, and that not only do sisters spend the most time together and provide the most support to one other, but they have the highest levels of conflict as well.[115]

Another factor that affects the sibling relationship is the extent to which the siblings share a genetic connection. In a German study of approximately 5,500 young adults, step-siblings who did not share a genetic connection with one another but are siblings through their parents' marriage were found to have relationships that are less engaged compared to the relationships between full genetic siblings.[116] This study also found that half-siblings, who share either a mother or a father, have relationships that are similar to those among full siblings, potentially because they share a genetic connection to one parent, or because they are more likely to have lived with one another in childhood.

There are other kinds of families in which brothers and sisters share a genetic connection to one another but do not typically grow up in the same household. In countries around the world, parents conceive their children using assisted reproductive technologies, using donated eggs, sperm or embryos to conceive a child. This path to parenthood is used by many different kinds of parents, such as those who are single, those who are in same-sex relationships and those who are in different-sex relationships who have experienced infertility or want to avoid passing on a genetic disease to their child.

The children in these families are genetically related to individuals in other families who have also been conceived using the same donor, who are often referred to as donor siblings.

If they are aware of the nature of how they were conceived, and if they are interested in doing so, donor-conceived individuals can try to find their donor relations. There is a website that helps people to do so – The Donor Sibling Registry, which was founded in 2000 by Wendy Kramer and her donor-conceived son, Ryan. In 2021, the registry had officially connected 21,000 people with their donor relations. To understand more about the relationship between donor siblings, I spoke with Wendy, who has decades' worth of experience in supporting donor-conceived individuals as they embark on finding their donor relations. She explained that these relationships unfold in different ways:

Donor family is something that people define for themselves. There's no right or wrong way to come at it. For some people they feel like acquaintances, for some people they feel like siblings, and for some people they feel like friends. It's not like any one of those ways is better or worse, or right or wrong, it's up to the people to define. Everyone takes this at a different speed and depth depending on their own personalities and comfort levels. With donor siblings there's more choice as to how the relationship will go. In many ways, donor family is no different than any other family. Some people you want to hang out with, some people you don't. It makes you no less genetically related to them if you don't like them or you don't want to spend time with them.

Although gender and genetic relatedness can often shape the quality of the relationships between brothers and sisters in adulthood, other factors play an important role, too. For example, relationships have been found to be closer between siblings who identify as heterosexual compared to those who identify as lesbian, gay or bisexual (LGB). In an Australian survey in which approximately 13,000 adults described the quality of their relationships with their siblings, those who identified as LGB had less face-to-face contact, less contact by email, letter or phone, and lived further apart from one another.[117] The authors of this study suggest that prejudice may be experienced by the LGB population within their families. The findings of other studies conducted in this field indicate that individuals who do not identify as heterosexual often perceive their parents and siblings as being unsupportive of their sexual orientation.

Although we often think of brothers and sisters as being close and having relationships that are active across the span of their lives, I have come to understand that, in reality, these relationships are varied and influenced by a broad range of factors. Although many people have active relationships with their brothers and sisters in which they see one another often, a substantial proportion do not. I have learnt that, just as there is no "normal" relationship between a parent and a grown child, there appears to be no "normal" relationship between siblings either.

What about twins?

Of all of the sibling relationships, it is the relationship between twins that is usually shown to be the closest. In films and television, twins are often depicted as sharing a special knowing or sixth sense about what is going in their brother's or sister's life. I was curious to know: Do twins in fact have a relationship that is set apart from those who are not twins?

While a lot of studies have been conducted on twins, not many explore the quality of their relationships with one another. Instead, studies focus on exploring questions relating to nature and nurture. Twins typically experience the same environment, growing up in the same home and being raised by the same parents, but it is only identical twins who share the same genes: non-identical twins are like any other siblings. Twins therefore present researchers with an ideal situation in which to test out questions about the extent to which our lives are determined by our genes and the extent to which they are influenced by the environment. Unfortunately, twins' experiences of their relationships with each other are therefore less well studied.

But of those studies that have explored the quality of the relationship between twins in adulthood, some have found that twin relationships are different from those between your average brother and sister.

For example, in a nationally representative sample of adults in the United States, approximately 28,000 adults completed a brief survey about the quality of their relationships with their siblings, of whom around 400 were twins.[118] The researchers found that twins were more likely to have what psychologists call an "attachment" relationship with each other compared to non-twins. Attachment relationships are those that we turn to in order to meet our deepest emotional needs. We turn to them for comfort in times of distress and for a sense of security that can enable us to explore the world around us, safe in the knowledge that someone will be there for us if and when we need them.

To learn more about the twin relationship, I sought out Dr Barbara Klein, an author who has written extensively about the challenges that twins face. I wanted to learn more about Dr Klein's experience as a clinical psychologist, working with those who experience challenges in their relationship with their twin. Dr Klein explained that it was the intense and special nature of the relationship between twins that can create disharmony. She explained:

I don't talk to twins who get along necessarily. And what I often hear is that it can be hard to stop the fighting. I can't tell you how many twins contact me and say, I read what you wrote. I think you really understand what I'm talking about. And this idea that fighting is common in twin relationships has helped me in my own life, because I'm a twin. My sister and I have fought our whole lives. Twin anger is very intense. There can be so much family fighting. Why can't we just have

Thanksgiving dinner and not fight? This is a big question. It's complicated and there is no one answer to that, but this is something that troubles people, that they can't get along.

There are different reasons why the twin relationship can be a challenging one. Twins share their parents and their childhood; this can breed competition and jealousy throughout their lives. My research indicates that twins have an identity as an individual and an identity as a twin, which can be problematic, because if they are too jealous or too competitive that can create problems. For twins, fighting, hostility and resentment is more present in young adulthood and middle age. I think middle age is often a time when twins want to get along but they often can't, especially if they hold onto the stories of how they hurt one another: "You did this and you did that".

In speaking with Dr Klein, I was surprised to hear that the twin relationship is one in which conflict can be prominent. I told her that my beliefs about twins had been shaped by the books that I had grown up with and the media more broadly, which tend to portray twin relationships as being particularly special and close. Dr Klein explained how the mythology that surrounds twins can be damaging, intensifying twin's feelings of shame when their relationship isn't in line with society's expectations:

I think the shame and embarrassment that comes with estrangement can be exponentially more difficult for twins because there is a mythology that twins should get along. In our culture, twins are an icon of idealized intimacy and when twins don't get along, they feel that there's something wrong with them. While twins feel humiliated and ashamed for not getting along, a part of them also wants to get along, so it can be a confusing situation.

I think that this is something I have learnt: that it's not always this great wonderful thing to be a twin. It's a complicated relationship. Some twins are close and some twins aren't. Another thing that I've learned is that twins can be so elated and relieved to know that other twins don't get along. That is the most significant finding of my research. It's the idea that other people have had that experience of not getting along and the pain that it can cause. When twins understand that they're not alone, that there are others who feel the same way, it can be extremely healing.

Dr Klein's perspective in working with hundreds of twins over many decades is a valuable one. And hopefully, over time, research on twin relationships in both childhood and adulthood will grow so that we can learn more about how these relationships unfold, in positive ways in addition to those that are more problematic. Hopefully, we can then gain a sense of what factors can strengthen these relationships, and how twins, parents and other siblings in the family can best be supported.

Research on the quality of the twin relationship in childhood is also sparse, but what we do know raises a number of interesting questions. For example, in one British study, parents reported on the quality of their children's relationships with one another in approximately 400 families. The study found that identical twins, non-identical twins and non-twins behaved towards one another in similar ways – that, unexpectedly, there were no substantial differences between the groups in terms of either the positive elements of the relationship, like companionship, sharing and affection, or the negative aspects, such as quarrels, competing and jealousy.[119] Given that some studies with adult twins have reached the opposite conclusion, the authors of this study suggested that it could be that twin relationships change in nature as twins grow older and spend more time outside of the family home.

While this field of study remains small, the research that does exist has already changed the way that I think about twins. I had often felt a gentle envy of those with a twin: that it must be a blessing to have someone in life who knows you so intimately, from before you were even born. And for some twins, this might well be the case. But what I have come to understand is that the twin relationship will not be experienced in that way by all. Contrary to what is suggested by the myths that we see on our screens, twins are not necessarily lifelong best friends and confidants who share a special bond over the course of their lives.

What happens when a parent dies?

In the family story, the love between family members is strong and enduring. It is more robust than other kinds of love, like that between friends. Presumably then, there are few events in life that will weaken this lifelong bond. I was therefore curious to know how the relationships between brothers and sisters are affected when a parent becomes frail, vulnerable or ill and requires care, and to find out what happens to this relationship when a parent dies. Is the sibling relationship so strong that it is unaffected by these events? Or does the sibling relationship weaken or break down when their parents are no longer there to hold it together?

What I have discovered is that when a parent becomes ill, frail or disabled in older age, conflict between brothers and sisters can arise. Siblings can often find themselves disagreeing when it comes to the distribution of care for a parent, and whether this distribution is fair. For example, in one study conducted in the United States of 100 children caring for parents or parents-in-law, 40 per cent were found to be having a relatively serious conflict with another family member over caregiving.[120] Those siblings who were more involved in providing care experienced frustration and anger towards those who were less involved. The authors of this study noted: "Some of these conflicts became so heated that relationships were severed or legal action taken."

Providing care for a parent can also be a time when parental favouritism can rear its head. For example, in another study conducted in the United States of 450 adult children, those who reported the greatest tension in the sibling relationships were those who perceived their mothers to favour a particular child as being their future caregiver.[121] Tension can also arise when siblings are on different pages regarding the nature and severity of their parent's illness and their need for care. In one study of a nationally representative sample of 861 adult child caregivers in the United States, the authors found that the different members of the family often disagreed about the nature and extent of their parent's need for care and how their parent should be cared for, which then led to family conflict.[122]

The second event that has the potential to cause conflict between siblings is when a parent dies. Surprisingly, relatively few studies have explored how issues relating to inheritance after a parent's death can affect the sibling relationship. To understand how and why this can be a challenging time for sibling relationships, I reached out to Professor Heather Conway at Queens University, Belfast, whose research focuses on different areas of law, such as family funeral disputes, and succession law, which pertains to how a person's assets are distributed after they have died. Professor Conway explained that the death of a parent can be a time when emotions run high within a family:

When it comes to family disputes over inheritance, the concept of being rational often goes out of the window because this is a time when family members are mourning the death of a loved one. As well as the grieving process, the death of a parent presents a massive shift in the internal family dynamics. Those emotions may distort or make compromise less likely and they can also bring power struggles to the fore. Death can bring out the best in people, but it can bring out the absolute worst as well.

The passing of a family member – this thing that is supposed to unite families and see people coming together – sometimes does absolutely nothing of the sort. Someone dies and it's a seismic shock within a family unit and it can implode a lot of family relationships, exposing old fault lines and dynamics that may have been bubbling under the surface. With the death of a family member you might get a cataclysmic event that brings it all to the fore.

Professor Conway went on to explain how these intense emotions can make the process of determining "who gets what" after a parent has died particularly difficult. She also told me that it is not just issues relating to inheritance that can cause conflict between siblings, but issues relating to funerals as well:

From my own research, and from speaking to funeral directors and people who work in a death profession you actually couldn't make up some of the family issues and conflicts that arise. There are often family rifts and fighting over funeral arrangements such as whether to bury or cremate and who controls the writing on the headstones. In a way it's less socially acceptable to be fighting over someone's funeral than their assets, but it's the same base level dynamics at play. When you have siblings fighting over a parent's estate they tend to take what one writer has called a "scorched earth" approach: nobody is going to have it, you fight until there is nothing left and everybody is unhappy. Some people have the mentality that "I will win anything at any cost."

Given that the death of a parent can be a time when old grievances come to the fore, it isn't surprising that Professor Conway and her colleagues often see a different side of family life than the one that we often see in adverts, on our social media platforms and on our screens. She explained:

What I have learnt in my work is that there is no one standard norm of expected behaviour. Families will never cease to amaze me. I'm not saying that all families are prone to infighting, bitterness and squabbles, but I think there is an underlying vulnerability in most, because in families people have different personalities, emotional attachments and relationship tensions. I think it's naive to assume that all families behave like a modified version of The Waltons, because they don't. I think there are more complicated families around than there are ideal fantasy families. And I think family relationships by their nature are complicated.

In speaking with Professor Conway, what I learnt is that a parent's death can affect the nature and the quality of sibling relationships in the short term, presenting brothers and sisters with opportunities for conflict. But studies have also explored how the death of a parent affects the sibling relationship over time. For example, in a nationally representative sample of approximately 4,000 adults in the Netherlands, researchers found that after both parents in the family died there was typically an increase in contact and conflict between siblings: however, over time, these relationships became more distant, leading them to conclude that: "sibling relations among adult orphans faded in the long run".[114]

I have spent so much time focusing on the early years of the sibling relationship, when brothers and sisters are children or adolescents, that I have given little thought to how these relationships change over time. But what I have come to appreciate is that caring for a parent at the end of life and managing a parent's estate can be emotional, stressful times in which conflict can arise and tensions can come to the fore. I have also learnt that the sibling relationship is one that appears to weaken once parents in the family have died. Sibling relationships do not exist in isolation, but rather are shaped by their parents in different ways. And this appears to be just as true when siblings are grown as it is when they are young.

When do siblings become estranged?

The assumption that sibling relationships are lifelong is so strong that very few researchers have focused on what happens when these relationships break down. When I set out to study estrangement, I knew very little about why it was that the relationships between brothers and sisters became distant and strained. I was therefore curious to know: how often do these relationships break down? And what kind of factors contribute to the estrangement between brothers and sisters?

Although I have not found definitive answers, I have found a number of helpful clues that are scattered across studies like breadcrumbs. Firstly, I found studies that suggested that estrangement between siblings isn't necessarily common, but that it isn't rare either. For example, in a sample of approximately 4,000 adults in the Netherlands, 13 per cent reported that they had had contact with their sibling no more than once in the past year.[114] And a similar figure emerged in a smaller sample of 262 adult siblings in the United States: one in 10 participants in this study had a troubled relationship with their siblings, ranging from relationships that were contentious to those in which there was no communication at all.[111] The authors of this study observed: "Just as music is defined by the silences and art by the space on the canvas, relationships with siblings can be defined by the absence of connection".

As for why estrangement occurs, researcher Dr Kylie Agllias explains that one route to relationship breakdown is "secondary estrangement". Given that we know so little about this kind of estrangement, I reached out to Dr Agllias to ask her to explain how and why this can happen. She explained:

> As the name suggests, a secondary estrangement results from a primary or initial family estrangement. So, my research suggests that when an estrangement occurs, some family members will take a strong position about who is right and wrong and align themselves with one party and estrange the other. Most family members will try to stay neutral for a period of time, or they might try to reason with the estranged parties. But as time goes on, most will take a position or feel compelled to "take sides". Basically, it is really difficult to stay in "no man's land" in a family, where trust, loyalty and similar values are expected.

Dr Agllias's explanation has allowed me to understand why an estrangement between a parent and a child in a family could then contribute to estrangement between siblings, with brothers and sisters feeling compelled to take sides. However, no studies have yet explored how common this path to estrangement between siblings is or what this experience might be like.

I found that another cause of estrangement is that of sibling abuse. For example, in one in-depth study exploring the experiences of 73 adult survivors of sibling incest and assault, 34 per cent did not have contact with their abusive sibling in adulthood.[104] And in a larger study of 4,500 German-speaking adults, those who had experienced emotional neglect in childhood were more likely to have a distant or a hostile relationship with their sibling in adulthood, characterized by low levels of warmth.[123]

In studying estrangement amongst family members more generally, I have come to appreciate that there is rarely one reason as to why a relationship breaks down. Family relationships are complex and messy, and so too are the factors that contribute to estrangement. This was certainly true for one woman I spoke to, Celia, who is estranged from her three brothers. Celia told me that the way that she thinks about her relationship with her brothers has not been simple or straightforward, but rather has taken a long time for her to understand. She explained:

> I had a good relationship with my parents when they were alive. My dad was a difficult man in some ways, although I loved him dearly. He was tough on all of us growing up, including my mother. And I was close with my mum always, she was such a levelling influence, but she had to put up with a lot from my dad. He would spank us with a belt and yell at us, and we were never really good enough. I can see now that he kind of set the tone for the family. There were ups and downs with my brothers, but back in those days I got along with them, or so I thought. As soon as I was old enough, I ran out of home, I had to get away. It was oppressive, I think all of us did. And it took me a while to figure that out.

Although Celia and her brothers grew up in a challenging family environment, it was not until many decades later that her relationship

How do sibling relationships survive in adulthood?

with her brothers began to deteriorate. She described this change in their relationship in the following way:

> As I grew older, my Dad came to appreciate and respect me in ways he hadn't when I was younger. In turn, I was able to enjoy the good things about him, and there were many. But whereas my relationship with my father got better, my relationship with my brothers got worse - and I don't blame my Dad for that. I really began to see the problems with my brothers once my parents needed care. That's when the gloves came off. I thought we were doing a good job of taking care of them; in some ways my brothers and I agreed about how to care for them, but in other significant ways we disagreed. And my brothers were furious with me for raising my concerns. There came a time when my brothers wouldn't discuss my mother's care with me, they shut down. And it's traumatizing to have someone that you care about so much but to have nobody who will hear it. When my mother needed care, I had such difficulty in actually getting access to her. My brothers wanted to have me ask permission to come over and see my mother, which was ridiculous. The control was absurd, I was not accepting of that. I thought to myself – I don't need to call to ask for permission to come and see my mother.

Celia told me that it was only really after her mother's death that she has come to understand the nature of her relationship with her brothers and how it has impacted her life. She explained:

207

I've been realizing a lot since my mother died. I think before she died, I was too immersed in it, like you can't see the forest for the trees. But I've had revelations since my mum has died and I've thought, how did I miss that? It's shocking. I've done a lot of reading about this just to try and help get me through this. And that's when I started realizing that this was rising to the level of abuse. I knew I would never accept this behaviour from anyone, nor would I dole it out. Occasionally when people get angry they might say things they shouldn't say, but it doesn't go on for years, it stops.

I have felt completely abandoned by my brothers, and they lie a lot. They even lie about things that don't matter. And the worst thing is, they won't admit it. They won't acknowledge any of what's happened. They won't speak to me about the problems we've gone through, so how can you get to resolution? Years ago, I had trust in them, but I have no trust in them whatsoever now. And they hacked my narrative, I couldn't even tell my own story. And that can take the life out of somebody. And in a way, I have had to forgive myself, because there's three of them, and one of me.

Celia's eloquent description allowed me to understand that the way that we think about our family relationships is far from static. It changes over time, sometimes slowly and sometimes all at once. And Celia touched on something else about the sibling relationship that seems so important too: that the way that her brothers treated her would be unacceptable in the context of other kinds of relationships. Celia went on to explain that just like estrangement between parents and children, estrangement between siblings is smothered in stigma, secrecy and shame:

> There are so few people that I can discuss this with, because it's not a comfortable topic. And people are sometimes so dismissive. But I have this hope, I had a glimpse after my mother died, that I hadn't had ever in my life, of what it will be like to not have my brothers constantly berating me. Because I've never been good enough, no matter what I do. I've had a glimpse of what life will be like without the constant lies and nastiness. And I think I'm going to feel better. I don't think I'm going to miss having contact with them, because for so many years, the contact has been fraught, so it will be a relief not to have it.

Although these kinds of experiences can be incredibly painful, for some, like Celia, being estranged from a sibling has the potential to bring relief. Given that the sibling relationship has been identified as being one of the most aggressive that most people experience over the course of their lives, I find it hard to understand why there is so little research about estrangement between siblings. And because there is so little research on this topic, it is difficult to make conclusions about the prevalence of sibling estrangement, its causes or its consequences. But from what we know so far, what we can conclude is that sibling relationships are not always lifelong: they both can, and do, break down.

The longest relationship of our lives?

Surprisingly, and frustratingly, I feel like I know less about the relationships between brothers and sisters in adulthood now than when I first set out to explore them. The researcher in me would very much like to wrap this chapter up in a tidy bow, but I have found that there is little research on sibling relationships in adulthood compared to those in childhood. It is no wonder, then, that the conclusions that I am trying to reach feel tentative.

· Although I have tried to explore a diverse range of sibling relationships, there are many other kinds of relationships between brothers and sisters that we rarely see on our screens. Just as some might learn that they have a half-sibling through sending off a seemingly innocuous saliva sample to a DNA company in the post, others might receive a phone call from a half-brother or half-sister who was conceived in a relationship prior to, or during, a parent's marriage. I have only just started to scratch the surface of the diversity and variation that exists within these relationships.

In doing so, I have learnt that these relationships function in different ways; that while some are characterized by weekly or monthly contact, a substantial proportion are not. I have also learnt that while we might think of twins as being particularly close, this

210

is not necessarily true for all. Importantly, I have come to appreciate that the myths that surround twin relationships are not just misleading, but harmful, increasing the chance that those who fall outside of these idyllic storylines of lifelong intimacy and connection will experience shame.

I have also come to appreciate that navigating care for a parent and settling an inheritance can be situations in which conflict is high in the sibling relationship. Of course, the opposite is possible too: that for some siblings, these events might provide opportunities for meaningful connection. Hopefully, research in the next decade and beyond can continue to help elucidate why it is that these events are more challenging for some than others, and how those who are experiencing challenge can best be supported.

There are many other areas where research on sibling relationships in adulthood is needed. For example, it would be interesting to know more about what it is like to navigate caring for a parent when sons or daughters are only children, as well as those families in which one child has an active relationship with their parent, but their siblings do not. In these families there is arguably a higher potential that children will experience feelings of burden, with a parent's care falling onto the shoulders of one child. However, it could also be possible that navigating the care of a parent could be simpler in these kinds of families compared to those in which brothers and sisters have to negotiate how a parent should be cared for, and who should provide it.

Although books and studies on sibling relationships start the same way – by explaining that it is our brothers and sisters who will know us for the longest period of our lives – with these lesson in mind, we can acknowledge that this is not true for all. And we can also begin to appreciate that for some, a distant, inactive relationship with a sibling will come as a relief that enables them to live their lives free from abuse and aggression.

These lessons, like many of the other lessons that I have learnt about family relationships, have the potential to be comforting. Those who have experienced pain, disconnection and heartache in a relationship with a brother or a sister will hopefully no longer feel that they are alone in this experience. And once again, there seems to be freedom in letting go of the story of how we think a family relationship should be: perhaps there isn't any one way that a relationship between a brother and sister should look after all?

nine

Changing the narrative: no family is perfect

If you have a voice, you have influence to spread,
if you have relationships, you have hearts to guide,
if you know young people, you have futures to mould,
if you have privilege, you have power to share,
if you have money, you have support to give,
if you have a ballot, you have policy to shape,
if you have pain, you have empathy to offer,
if you have freedom, you have others to fight for,
if you are alive, you are a leader.

Abby Wambach, *Wolfpack*[124]

Although they might seem bleak at first glance, I am incredibly grateful for the lessons that I have learnt about family. Because despite the fact that families are often depicted as being strong, stable and safe, what I now know is that people have all kinds of different experiences in their family relationships. When it comes to family, there are no two the same. Families and family relationships are endlessly complex.

Yet within this messiness, there is one important way in which all families are alike: no family is perfect, free from pain, change or growth. Even if a relationship seems fairly simple at one moment in time, no one has the ability to wrap it up and put it in the attic to gather dust. As time passes, life happens: there will be births, deaths, marriages, miscarriages and divorces, along with mental and physical health problems, addictions, accidents and illnesses. And an inevitable consequence of change is loss: sometimes the loss of the status quo, but at other times the loss of a relationship entirely. And it is in this way that we are all connected. As Dr Maya Angelou concluded in her poem "Human Family", "We are more alike, my friends, than we are unalike".[125]

I can now see how the family story that I grew up with led me astray. I now understand that the rigid categories that I once used to navigate the world – sorted, failing, good, bad – are inadequate, and that the fairytale narratives of how families should be fuel feelings of separation and shame. Because when we buy into the myth that family relationships are easy and uncomplicated, strong and enduring, it is inevitable that we will feel less-than when we experience the range of human, complex emotions that occur in relationships between human beings.

In this final chapter we will explore how we all stand to benefit when we change the narrative of the family story. These final lessons are suggestions as to how we might accomplish meaningful, lasting change that can benefit us all, regardless of what we have experienced in our family relationships.

Acknowledge those who lack supportive family relationships

In the family story, it is family members who share the strongest love of all; the love between family members is natural, unconditional and unchanging. According to this story, those whose relationships do not fit this narrative are the pieces of the puzzle that do not fit. So how should we respond to those who experience pain and rejection in their family relationships? Is it their responsibility, and theirs alone, to forgive and forget and to mend what has been broken? Or do we have the ability to support those who do not have family relationships in which they feel safe and loved?

Some might argue that people can experience deep and meaningful love in different ways; it does not need to be found in relationships with those with whom we share genes, childhoods or surnames. People create meaningful, significant connections through civil partnerships and marriage, just as they can invest in long-lasting, supportive relationships with friends or join welcoming communities. In my own life I have certainly experienced family to be a creative act.

And yet, while it is true that we can create our own support networks in life, it is also true that our relationships with our parents, siblings and children matter. A recent review of research on family relationships concluded that the quality of the relationships that we have with our parents, adult children and siblings are related to our general feelings of happiness, life satisfaction and mental and physical health.[126] Supportive relationships, in which family members offer one another love, care and practical assistance, are protective, lessening the impact of stressful life events on our health. On the other hand, family relationships can be a source of strain; those relationships in which there are high levels of conflict, demandingness and criticism have a negative impact on well-being over the course of our lives.

Family relationships also matter because, in general, these relationships appear to have a solidity that other kinds of relationships often lack. For example, in a study of 37,000 people in Germany that was conducted over a 15-year period, the frequency of visits between family members was found to remain constant, yet visits with friends became less frequent over time.[3] This pattern was especially true in times of need. When people experienced poor health, the frequency of visits with family members remained unaffected, but the frequency of visits with friends lessened over time.

Other large-scale studies have found a similar pattern. In an analysis of 277 studies, comprising data from approximately 180,000 participants, the size of people's family networks tended to remain stable across the life span. Yet, in contrast, the size of people's friendship networks peaked from their twenties to their mid-thirties and then declined across the later stages of adulthood and into older age.[127]

Researchers explain these patterns with reference to the goals that people have at the different stages of their lives. Adolescence and early adulthood are times of exploration when people typically seek out new friendships, whereas in adulthood and older age, people tend to focus on a smaller number of close relationships. Family relationships are also described as being inherently different to friendship. Whereas friendships are typically characterized by balance and reciprocity, these qualities are less important in a family relationship, as it is assumed these bonds can be activated in times of need, such as in a health emergency. In this way – in theory, at least – family relationships are less affected by the notion of give and take, and more likely to act as a safety net that is ready to catch family members, if and when they fall.

But while we know that family matters, we also know from research on estrangement that family relationships do not always function as a safety net. And when we acknowledge that family relationships are not necessarily lifelong or supportive, we are then able to determine whether actions can be taken to support people who find themselves in ones that are not. The question of how to support people experiencing estrangement is one that drives the work of the charity Stand Alone, which was initiated by Dr Becca Bland in 2014. I spoke with Dr Bland and asked her to tell me about how the charity began. She told me:

Back in 2012 I wrote a personal piece about my own estrangement from family. I hadn't really seen anybody write about this before and I wrote it around Christmas, when I think there's a lot of stigma for people who don't have contact with their family. When that was published, I got so many responses from people saying that they had never heard or seen anybody write about this before and that they thought they were the only ones going through it. They wrote to tell me that it had really helped them to see someone else that was in the same situation.

I thought, Wow, this is really interesting, there are so many people here who think they are the only people in the situation, just like I had. And I met one of those people who lived two streets down from me. We had a coffee and we talked about the similarities in our experience. And the relief I felt from just that one very informal coffee was amazing. I felt like something had lifted. I wasn't alone. And that was the start of Stand Alone.

Stand Alone has shone a light on the experiences of students who are estranged from their parents. In the UK, students who are 25 or younger who apply for loans are required to provide information about their parents' income. This policy is one in which the family story is alive and kicking, as it has been developed on the assumption that parents will contribute to the costs that their sons and daughters incur while studying. Students who do not have a supportive relationship with their parents therefore need to submit evidence to prove that they are estranged from them. This currently involves submitting a signed letter from a social worker, doctor or teacher who is willing to attest to the estrangement. Given that estrangement is something that few people want to share with other people due to the shame and judgement that surrounds it, this can be a challenging process for students, especially when they have experienced abuse. Dr Bland told me what she hoped this system could look like in the future:

In an ideal world I would love for students to be able to apply for the student loan without having to go through a traumatic process to prove that they don't have those family relationships. To encounter such stressful processes when you have experienced trauma in your family is an infringement on people's rights. And from the very start I would wish for the language in the guidance and advice to acknowledge that their situation isn't abnormal, but rather that this is what family life is like for some people. There are so many areas of policy that are badly planned around family due to presumptions of the ideal family, and this is one area where our work has made concrete, meaningful change.

As Dr Bland makes clear, the reality of family relationships needs to be reflected and embedded in both policy and practice. The work of the charity Stand Alone proves that there are actions that can be taken to support people who are estranged from their family members. And there are many other areas of policy and practice that would likewise benefit from recognizing that assumptions about family relationships are just that – assumptions – and that, in reality, there is great diversity in the ways that family relationships function. But if we are to engage with those difficult, challenging questions as to how to initiate meaningful change in policy, a vital first step is to acknowledge that the family story is a myth that has more in common with a fairytale than it does with reality.

Know that people can overcome challenging family relationships and thrive

In writing this book I have delved into the research on adversity and trauma. Not only are these fields of research complex, but initially, on first sight, they seem to suggest inevitable doom: that those who have experienced hardship are going to struggle in life. At the start of writing this book, I thought of some of the events that had unfolded in the branches of my own family tree with a certain heaviness.

However, as I come to the end of writing this book, I find myself feeling more hopeful than ever. What I now know is that change isn't just possible, but that it is an essential part of what it means to be human. In one extensive review of research on child development, the authors concluded: "Human development is not predetermined, fixed, or linear; it is not prefigured in a genetic program. Rather, it is unique to each and every individual, highly responsive to environments, cultures, and relationships, continuously adapting, organizing, and reorganizing, and subject to change across the lifespan".[128] If I apply this quote to my own life, I can conclude that nothing about my future is fixed or certain, and that I have the ability to actively seek out supportive relationships and experience change, growth and progress.

So how can those who have experienced challenges in their family relationships best be supported to overcome them and thrive? A rich field of research in psychology is the development of interventions to help support and improve family relationships, most of which are aimed at parents who are raising young children. These interventions vary: some are delivered online and others in the family home; some run for one month and others for two years; some focus on educating family members, and in others trained professionals give feedback on the ways that family members interact with one another.

Many of these interventions have been shown to improve different aspects of the relationships between parents and their children. The authors of a recent review of interventions explain that they can improve the way that parents help children recognize and label their emotions; the way that parents engage in conflict and handle challenging behaviour in a constructive way; and parents' ability to recognize how important it is for them to care for themselves.[129] They conclude: "Certainly, a goal of our field might be to normalize parent education to the extent that it would be unusual to not want to learn more about one of the most important relationships in life."

Parenting interventions can improve various facets of the relationships between parents and children, and they can be particularly effective when parents are facing significant challenges. I spoke with Professor Helen Minnis a Professor of Child and Adolescent Psychiatry at the University of Glasgow in the UK, whose research has focused on the effects of early abuse on children's development. She explained:

We're doing this intervention for families for whom a judge has said that parents have abused or neglected their children and the

223

child has been removed and come into foster care. The families are randomly allocated into a mental health intervention or to social work. What's really interesting is that one of my colleagues working on the team said what she's really noticed, just in a few weeks of working with these families, was that actually the parents were just trying to do their best. Sometimes parents are misguided, it's not that they're bad or stupid, not at all.

A lot of people have been taught "spare the rod, spoil the child" – that if they don't hit hard enough, they should hit harder, or their children will grow up to be spoilt. And some of these parents, when it's explained to them that what they're doing is not helping, it's harming, many of these parents are like, woah, can you give me help? They're often in really difficult situations and they're trying their best to turn it around. Those are the people I think are heroes, I really do.

In addition to interventions that are focused on improving or strengthening family relationships, it is also helpful to focus on helping people outside of the context of their families. Many organizations strive to create meaningful change in people's lives through the creation of new, supportive relationships that can bring a message of hope and optimism into young people's lives. For example, Smash Life is a UK organization that offers mentoring, group work and motivational talks for children and young people growing up in the care system, which is something that founders Matt and Andy Smith have experienced themselves. One of the tag lines of their company is: "Let the past make you better – not bitter". Andy explained why a central aspect of their work is giving children the message of hope:

> Some educational materials show that if you've grown up in an abusive or challenging environment, you're going to follow in the footsteps of those who came before you. I was very uncomfortable when I saw a video on adverse childhood experiences at a conference. I spoke up and I said that we just need to give a bit more hope, because every child has potential. Sometimes you just need to open up your mindset. Because you can't get away from it, it's horrible to hear about some of the journeys that some of the children are going through in the UK care system. But then you've got to show up for them with that mindset of being that person in their life that can make them believe that they can look to the future and feel hopeful.

As Andy suggests, a key ingredient to making positive change is supportive relationships. This message is key not just in psychology but also in the fields of social work, neuroscience and public health. For example, in their book *What Happened to You?: Conversations on Trauma, Resilience, and Healing*, psychiatrist and neuroscientist Dr Bruce Perry and Oprah Winfrey explain the power of supportive relationships in this way: "your history of relational health – your connectedness to family, community, and culture – is more predictive of your mental health than your history of adversity ... connectedness has the power to counterbalance adversity".[130]

While it is important to focus on the creation of supportive relationships, it is important to think of the bigger picture too. There are many different areas of policy that can have a real and lasting impact on people's lives and on the quality of their family relationships. For example, in a comprehensive review of family policy in the United States, family policy consultant Theodora Ooms explains that numerous policies have the power to affect families in direct and indirect ways. For example, she explains that since the introduction of a national system of daycare centres in the early 1970s, it is now widely accepted that mothers work outside the home, and that families benefit from childcare subsidies and flexible work schedules.[81] However, she also stresses that there is still a long way to go: high quality childcare is not accessible to all, and the United States remains the only major industrialized country that does not provide paid family leave when a child is born.

Whether it is in the development of interventions, the curation of supportive relationships or the enactment of family policy, change is possible. And not only that – change is possible whether people face mild, moderate or severe challenges in their family relationships. Although it is not necessarily quick or easy, people can overcome challenging family relationships and thrive.

But there is an important barrier that gets in the way of change, which is the family story – the way that we think families should be. In the review described above, Theodora Ooms describes that, within politics, denial is common. She puts it this way: "In my view…there is a tendency to sugar-coat family issues – to describe families always in saccharine terms and fail to openly acknowledge the ambivalent feelings and dark sides of family life". She goes on to explain why it is that the denial, minimization and avoidance of talking about families as they actually are, rather than how they could or should be, is so common: "It may be easier to avoid discussions about family policy because they may open up many mixed and ambivalent feelings that are uncomfortable to deal with."

However, we need not fear those "mixed and ambivalent feelings" that can arise when we talk about families as they are, rather than as they could or should be. That is exactly what we have done in the chapters of this book, and we are still here, breathing in and out.

When it comes to family, there is so much to gain in changing the narrative. When we think of the love between family members as natural, instinctive and perfect, it requires no effort; there is nothing to learn, and there is no need to intervene. But when we think of the love between family members as being like all other kinds of love – flawed, human and messy – the opposite is true: we can make an effort, there is a need to intervene and there are ways that families can be supported. Ultimately, what I have learnt is this: change and progress are possible when it comes to family relationships, but only when the family is taken off its pedestal.

Appreciate that people heal from challenging family relationships in different ways

People who have experienced hurt in their family relationships are often told to let bygones be bygones. Likewise, those who are estranged from family members are encouraged to "pick up the phone and call them". Is forgiveness the best and only path to healing from challenging family relationships? Or it is sometimes better, and safer, to walk away?

Forgiveness is broadly understood to refer to the decision to let go of negative, resentment-based emotions, thoughts and behaviours and to develop positive regard for the person who has wronged or harmed you, like compassion. Not only is forgiveness a pillar of religions and spiritual paths and practices around the world, but it has a growing evidence base. For example, a recent analysis of the findings of 15 studies concluded that forgiveness interventions reduce common mental health problems such as depression, stress and distress and promote positive emotions.[131]

However, forgiveness is far from simple. In a review of three studies of forgiveness interventions in the context of women who had experienced abuse, the authors concluded that forgiveness can be an effective way of improving psychological and physical health.[132] However, in reaching this conclusion, the authors clarified exactly what forgiveness is and what it isn't. Specifically, they provided the following points of clarification: that forgiveness does not mean the offence or the pain that it caused is excused or denied; that forgiveness is distinct from reconciling, forgetting, pardoning and accepting; that a survivor of any type of abuse should not be encouraged to forgive their abuser until they are safe and removed from the abusive environment; and that forgiveness takes time.

The distinction between forgiveness and reconciliation is one that psychologist Dr Harriet Lerner makes clear in her book, *Why Won't You Apologize? Healing Big Betrayals and Everyday Hurts*. She writes: "Accepting an apology doesn't always mean reconciliation. The best apology in the world can't restore every connection. The words 'I'm sorry' may be absurdly inadequate even if sincerely offered. Sometimes the foundation of trust on which a relationship was built cannot be repaired. We may never want to see the person who hurt us again. We can still accept the apology".[133]

As Dr Lerner explains, forgiveness is not the same as reconciliation; to forgive someone doesn't mean that you have to continue having an active relationship with them. For those who have survived abuse by a family member, reconciliation might be neither appropriate nor safe. And although we hear of this experience rarely, survivors of abuse might have the option of pursuing legal justice against their abusive family member. While there are substantial barriers to doing so, there can be significant benefits too. I asked Dino Nocivelli, a solicitor who specializes in child abuse, to explain why people decide to pursue legal justice and how it can affect their lives:

The pursuit of legal justice through the criminal and civil courts can be difficult and re-traumatizing. However, the process is also often described as being cathartic by survivors as it gives them an opportunity to be heard. Often survivors say they want to obtain justice and closure from the legal justice system, but others want things such as their family accepting that the abuse took place; perpetrators accepting blame for the abuse happening; or their loved ones appreciating the impact that abuse has had on their lives. Here in the UK, the civil justice system can sometimes help fund much-needed therapy, which can help people to address what happened to them with a view to making things better going forward for themselves and their family.

There is a saying that it takes a village to raise a child and I have always believed that it takes a village to abuse a child too. Often the abuser has not only groomed and abused a child but also their family members and members of the local community, thereby affecting everyone associated with the survivor. By disclosing their abuse, survivors can enable an open discussion that might mean protection of others from the abuser, and importantly an opportunity to reset the narrative within a family.

Dino's eloquent description has allowed me to understand that people choose to address the abuse that they have experienced in their family relationships in different ways. In learning these lessons, the way that I think about forgiveness and reconciliation has changed. I have come to appreciate that just as family relationships are diverse and complex, so too are people's paths to living with them or healing from them.

Talk about families in a different way

When people talk about family, they usually focus on the positives. They praise those family members with whom they have relationships that they value, and they express gratitude for what it is that they have. But is there a middle ground when it comes to talking about family? While we express appreciation for those relationships and experiences that we are grateful for, can we also share the more challenging experiences of family life that we have encountered?

I used to think that it was disloyal to speak about family in a way that was anything other than glowing and full of praise. One of the reasons why talking about family in a more nuanced, balanced way can feel like airing dirty laundry is that we hear people do this so rarely. Finding examples of people talking about the difficulties in their family relationships, not just the joys, can be hard.

But what I have learnt is that talking about the good experiences of family life alongside the bad is considered to be a sign of healthy psychological functioning. I often think of the words that Professor Miriam Steele, Co-Director of the School for Attachment Research at the New School in New York, said to me at the start of my journey of writing this book. She explained:

Ideally, as a researcher who studies attachment, what we're looking for is the ability for somebody to acknowledge the difficulties as well as what was good. As an analogy, we hear a lot these days about gratitude. But I think the other side of gratitude is recognizing those things that didn't go so well. You can be grateful for a change that happened, for all the good things that we might experience, but to be really meaningful and powerful, that appreciation has to be in the context of also acknowledging difficulties. Being able to talk about the good experiences and the bad is a much more balanced and enriching way of thinking and engaging with the world.

I have found this explanation to be both helpful and reassuring. But we do not just face the question of how we talk about our families to those we trust and feel safe with; we also face the question as to how we should present our family relationships to the outside world. We present our family relationships to the world in different ways: when we are out with family members in public places, when strangers ask us about our family relationships and when we send cards at the holidays. And this performative aspect of family life seems especially challenging in the changing landscape of social media.

Although the question as to how we should present our family relationships to the world is something that we all have to navigate, it can be particularly difficult to know how to do so when we are experiencing a challenging situation or loss. This complexity was captured by Gareth, a father of two young boys whose wife had recently died of cancer. Gareth told me:

People say to me all the time, "You're doing a fantastic job", "You're such a good dad", "You make it look so easy" and I don't feel any of those things. I don't feel like it's easy, I don't feel like I'm a fantastic dad; I feel like I'm going day to day from one moment to another, my eldest wanting his own bedroom, my youngest not doing his homework, all the things I've never dealt with before, that are suddenly cropping up on me now. I find it very difficult. I find it very stressful. And the hardest thing about being a sole parent is that you don't have anybody.

I do look on Facebook and Instagram and I have an account, I'm not very active on it but I use it as a way to let people know how we're doing. I wish people weren't so fake about how happy they are, I find it very strange, but then I guess I am one of those people. I'm not fake as in I'm not trying to make things look better than they are, but I definitely hide the fact that when things are bad, that when I'm feeling low or we're all not getting along, which happens, I don't make people aware of that.

A massive thing for me is people saying, "Oh aren't you doing well, the boys are happy." It makes me feel like my wife is forgotten now, and me and the boys are just the norm really and not a lot of thought goes into how we are coping. But then again, at the same time, when people ask me how I'm doing I say, "Alright". I don't know. I find it such a difficult thing.

Gareth did share with me one particularly powerful instance in which sharing the details of his family life fostered connection, empathy and support.

> It was October and I was taking the boys to school – I'd bought the new uniforms, and they'd worn shorts all through summer, and Louise used to get shorts or trousers out depending on what the weather was like. And we were walking to school and I realized my kids were the only kids in the shorts and everyone else wasn't and I felt like a bit of a failure, I said to the boys, "Oh. My. God. Everyone is in trousers and you two are still in your shorts." And my son said, "Why don't we just carry on wearing them?" and I said, "You can do if you want, why don't we do it for charity?". So we set up a JustGiving page for a local hospice, and local stations got hold of the story, a reporter came to the house and filmed the story, and it just went from £700 that night to about £5,000. Today they've raised £32,000. It's a strange thing but it probably got us through, it's kept us busy all the time and they're still wearing shorts now.

Many of us will relate to Gareth's thoughts as to how to present his family life on social media, and his example of transforming a moment of shame into a moment of connection and growth is a beautiful one. There will be times when the way that we talk about or present our family life and relationships won't be straightforward. Just as family relationships are complex, so too are the ways that we choose to present them to the outside world. But what I have learnt is that talking about a challenging experience isn't an indicator of weakness. Rather, to reflect on the good and the bad is, as Professor Steele put it, "a more balanced and enriching way of thinking and engaging with the world."

Embrace the messiness

Although they have not been easy or straightforward, I am grateful for the lessons that I have learnt about family. They have allowed me to develop a kinder voice in my head when I think about families: both other people's and my own.

So many of us want our families to be a soothing balm or a safe haven into which to retreat in times of trouble. And families certainly have the capacity to be and offer that, providing a space in which we feel seen, heard, valued and loved. But they are also a place of trauma, pain, silence and disconnection. I have learnt that experiences of adversity, abuse, aggression and estrangement are far from rare in family relationships. And I have gained a vocabulary that helps me to understand my own experiences and those of the people I love.

Although I didn't grow up watching his programmes, the words of the American children's entertainer Fred Rogers strike me as being particularly relevant when thinking about these difficult experiences in family relationships that are steeped in silence and stigma. He said: "Anything that's human is mentionable, and anything that is mentionable can be more manageable. When we can talk about our feelings, they become less overwhelming, less upsetting, and less scary. The people we trust with that important talk can help us know that we are not alone."[134]

I am also grateful to have learnt that feelings of frustration, disconnection and pain are not only experienced in "bad", "fractured" or "broken" families. They happen in all families, at different times, for all sorts of reasons. They are to be expected. Family relationships are by their very nature complex. Experiencing hurt and pain in a relationship with a parent, child or sibling does not infer weakness of character, or fault. Rather, experiencing pain in a family relationship makes us human, just like everyone else. No one's family or family relationships are perfect, free from pain, change or challenge.

The psychologist Dr Harriet Lerner reminds us that if we are human, experiencing pain is inevitable. She explains: "Countless self-help books, blogs and seminars promise relief from suffering, when pain and suffering are as much part of life as happiness and joy. The only way to avoid being mistreated in this world is to fold up in a dark corner and stay mute. If you go outside, or let others in, you'll get hurt many times. Ditto if you've grown up in a family rather than being raised by wolves. Some people will behave badly and will not apologize, repair the harm, or care about your feelings".[133]

I have also come to understand that different family members tend to see their relationships with each other in different ways. I have learnt that parents are more likely to have a rose-tinted view of the parent–child relationship and to be more invested in the relationship than their children. And I have also learnt that although a parent might say that they love a child, a child might not feel loved, and that it is a child's feelings of acceptance or rejection that can affect their well-being over the course of their life.

Rather than thinking of the love between family members as being the strongest and the most enduring love, for everyone, unquestioningly, I now think of family love like all other loves: joyful and painful, fleeting and enduring, fragile and robust. I now know that rather than simply painful or easy, the love between family members can be many things. It sours, and it spills; it shimmers, and it shines.

And these lessons that I have learnt have not just been an intellectual exercise. These lessons have changed the way that I feel about my own family experiences. In chapter one I reflected on the fact that my own family tree contains relationships that are warm and supportive, those that are distant, and those that are high in conflict. The facts of my family haven't changed as I have written this book but the way that I understand them has.

I can now appreciate that my experiences of family relationships do not lend themselves to a neat categorization of "good" or "bad", but reflect the complex pain and beauty of being a human being who loves and is loved by other human beings. At times I have compared my small potted plant to the epic oak trees of other people's families, which has led me to feel separate from, and less than, those around me. I know now that the fact that the branches of my family tree have been touched by mental health problems, estrangements and a drive towards a better life does not make me less-than. They make me just like everyone else. I have been more fortunate than others and I have been less fortunate than others. And, perhaps most unexpectedly, I have experienced a growing sense of gratitude for the more painful experiences that I have gone through and the person that I have become as a result.

I have also come to appreciate the value in acknowledging, rather than denying, my own experiences of pain, as well as the pain of other people. In doing so, I have developed the ability to care for myself deeply when I experience pain. And I have learnt that the more compassion that I can give to myself in feeling these emotions, the more easily I can extend it to others. I am grateful to have found this gentler, softer place for myself when I think about my own family experiences. I can be a little kinder, to myself and others, as I navigate love, in all of its different forms.

Although I have mostly recovered from the shame that comes from falling outside of the family story, I can sometimes get pulled back into its judgements. That daydreaming girl lost in the world of the perfect family is very much a part of me still. But I can now appreciate that when I get dragged into thinking that family relationships should be simple and idyllic in every moment of every day, I am being drawn into the family story, which pales in comparison to the kaleidoscope of feelings and experiences that happen when we live and love.

And thankfully, when I do get pulled back into the shame that accompanies the family story, I no longer live there. I no longer live in a place where I feel less-than. And I know that a life in which love that is perfect and performed is not a life I want to lead. I am grateful to have taken the narratives of the family story, to have held them up to the light, and to have let them go. Because what I now know is that that no family is perfect. And when it comes to family, there is no them and us. There is only us.

ACKNOWLEDGEMENTS

I am so grateful to have been surrounded by love whilst writing this book. Thank you to Sarah F and Sooz, my secure base and safe haven, who infuse my life with joy and kindness. Thank you to Sam and Sarah for our bubble of hugs, brownies and breakfast in the car. Mum and Dad, thank you for giving me a childhood unlike your own, for gently but persistently encouraging me to pursue my education, and for always telling me that my future is bright. Thank you to Neville who kept my feet warm as I wrote this book and for being such a good dog. Thank you to Donna, for shaping the person I am today and for believing in this book. Thank you to Rob for your support and for listening to me talk about this book while navigating a series of stressful roundabouts in Sicily back in 2019. Thank you to my Cedar Farmers, Billy, John and Paul (and Abel), Katie B and Ed and Kate O F, for all of the laughter, love and sticky toffee pudding. For her unwavering support and enthusiasm, thank you to Nicole. And thank you to the younger people in my life who fill my heart with love and hope: Ben and Emma; Ben and Zara; Edie and Evan; Josie and Luca; Little G, little T (and little D); Robyn and Marley; and Rueben and Hermione.

I am also grateful to have received many wonderful snacks while writing this book, especially when deadlines were looming. Thank you to John for leaving such a substantial wedge of my favourite carrot cake on my doorstep; to Sam for dropping off two weeks' worth of home-cooked meals when I needed it most; and to Sarah F and Sooz for sending me brownies that arrived on the same day, with almost identical messages of support inside.

The practical support that I received while writing this book was an enormous help. For reading drafts of chapters, I'd like to thank Axel, Cat M, Ed, John, Katie B, Katie C, Lucy, Paul and Sam. For those who read multiple drafts of many chapters, especially Sarah F and Sooz, I am eternally grateful. For reading the book in its entirety once it was drafted, thank you to Bernie, Joshua, Michael and Susan. Thank you to Bernie for your help with the diagram in chapter 3. For helping me to navigate contracts, thank you to Rob, Sam and Susan.

This book would not exist without the encouragement and patience of my agent, Esmond: thank you for seeing something in me and for believing in this book. I am also incredibly grateful for the thoughtful insights of my editor, Oli: thank you for giving me such helpful feedback in a kind and sensitive way. Thank you to Rachel for her diligent copy-editing. And thank you to the team at Welbeck for contributing to this book's journey.

Many people have supported me in pursuing my career. Susan – thank you for showing me how to be a kind, ambitious woman who nurtures those around her. I am also grateful to my colleagues at the Centre for Family Research, which was always a warm environment in which to learn and grow. Becca, thank you for your friendship, collaboration and support. I am also grateful for the support and friendship of my colleagues at Edge Hill, especially Axel, Bernie, Cat W, Kate and Lucy.

To the experts that I interviewed while writing this book, thank you for giving me your time and insight. And last but by no means least, I am grateful to those who have shared their experiences of family life with me: thank you for your courage. It has been an honour to have listened to you and to have learnt from you.

REFERENCES

1. Gillis JR. Our imagined families: The myths and rituals we live by. 2002. Emory Center for Myth and Ritual in American Life Working Paper Working Paper, 7(2).

2. Bowen M. Theory in the practice of psychotherapy. Family Therapy: Theory and Practice. 1976;4(1):2–90.

3. Sander J, Schupp J, Richter D. Getting together: Social contact frequency across the life span. Developmental Psychology. 2017;53(8):1571–88. http://doi.org/10.1037/dev0000349.

4. Guo M, Stensland M, Li M, Dong X. Parent–adult child relations of Chinese older immigrants in the United States: Is there an optimal type? The Journals of Gerontology: Series B . 2020;75(4):889–98. https://doi.org/10.1093/geronb/gbz021

5. Dykstra PA, Fokkema T. Relationships between parents and their adult children: A West European typology of late-life families. Ageing & Society. 2011;31(4):545–69. https://doi.org/10.1017/S0144686X10001108

6. Guo, M, Chi, I, & Silverstein, M. The structure of intergenerational relations in rural China: A latent class analysis. Journal of Marriage and Family. 2012. 74(5), 1114-1128. http://doi.org/10.1111/j.1741-3737.2012.01014.x

7. Silverstein M, Bengtson VL. Intergenerational solidarity and the structure of adult child–parent relationships in American families. American Journal of Sociology. 1997;103(2):429–60.

8. Kim K, Birditt KS, Zarit SH, Fingerman KL. Typology of parent–child ties within families: Associations with psychological well-being. Journal of Family Psychology. 2020;34(4): 448–58. https://doi.org/10.1037/fam0000595

9. Felitti VJ, Anda RF, Nordenberg D, Williamson DF, Spitz AM, Edwards V, et al. Relationship of childhood abuse and household dysfunction to many of the leading causes of death in adults: The adverse childhood experiences (ACE) study. American Journal of Preventative Medicine. 1998;14(4):245–58. https://doi.org/10.1016/S0749-3797(98)00017-8

10. Hughes K, Bellis MA, Hardcastle KA, Sethi D, Butchart A, Mikton C, et al. The effect of multiple adverse childhood experiences on health: a systematic review and meta-analysis. The Lancet Public Health. 2017;2(8):e356–66. http://dx.doi.org/10.1016/S2468-2667(17)30118-4

11. Bellis MA, Hughes K, Ford K, Ramos Rodriguez G, Sethi D, Passmore J. Life course health consequences and associated annual costs of adverse childhood experiences across Europe and North America: a systematic review and meta-analysis. The Lancet Public Health. 2019;4(10):e517–28. https://doi.org/10.1016/S2468-2667(19)30145-8

12. Purewal, SK, Bucci, M, Gutiérrez Wang, L, Koita, K, Silvério Marques, S, Oh, D, & Burke Harris, N. (2016). Screening for adverse childhood experiences (ACEs) in an integrated pediatric care model. Zero to three, 37(1), 10–17.

13. Van der Kolk BA. The body keeps the score: Brain, mind, and body in the healing of trauma. New York and London: Penguin Books; 2015.

14. Lacey RE, Minnis H. Practitioner review: Twenty years of research with adverse childhood experience scores – Advantages, disadvantages and applications to practice. Journal of Child Psychology and Psychiatry. 2020;61(2):116–30. https://doi.org/10.1111/jcpp.13135

15. Tedeschi RG, Shakespeare-Finch J, Taku K, Calhoun LG. Posttraumatic growth: Theory, research, and applications. New York: Routledge; 2018.

16. Sissay L. Gold from the stone: New and Selected poems. Edinburgh: Canongate Books Ltd; 2017.

17. Oliver M. Thirst. Boston, MA: Beacon Press; 2006.

18. Stand Alone. The prevalence of family estrangement. 2014;4. Available from: http://standalone.org.uk/wp-content/uploads/2013/08/StandAlonePrevalenceRESEARCH3.pdf

19. Coleman J. The Rules of estrangement: Why adult children cut ties and how to heal the conflict. New York: Harmony; 2021.

20. Agllias K. Family estrangement: A matter of perspective. London and New York: Taylor & Francis; 2016.

21. Lerner H. The dance of intimacy: A woman's guide to changing the patterns of intimate relationships. New York: HarperCollins; 1989.

22. Leijdesdorff S, Van Doesum K, Popma A, Klaassen R, Van Amelsvoort T. Prevalence of psychopathology in children of parents with mental illness and/or addiction: An up to date narrative review. Current Opinion in Psychiatry. 2017;30(4):312–17. https://doi.org/10.1097/YCO.0000000000000341

23. Fox AB, Earnshaw VA, Taverna EC, Vogt D. Conceptualising and measuring mental illness stigma: The mental illness stigma framework and critical review of measures. Stigma and Health. 2018;3(4):348–76. https://doi.org/10.1037/sah0000104

24. Slater L. Playing house: Notes of a reluctant mother. Boston, MA: Beacon Press; 2013.

25. Taraban L, Shaw DS. Parenting in context: Revisiting Belsky's classic process of parenting model in early childhood. Developmental Review. 2018;48, 55–81. Available from: https://doi.org/10.1016/j.dr.2018.03.006

26. Forslund T, Granqvist P, van IJzendoorn MH, Sagi-Schwartz A, Glaser D, Steele M, et al. Attachment goes to court: Child protection and custody issues. Attachment and Human Development. 2021 1–52. https://doi.org/10.1080/14616734.2020.1840762

27. Khaleque A, Ali S. A systematic review of meta-analyses of research on interpersonal acceptance–rejection theory: Constructs and measures. Journal of FamilyTheory and Review. 2017;9(4):441–58. http://doi.org/10.1111/jftr.12228

28. Nomaguchi, K. & Milkie, M. A. Parenthood and well-being: A decade in review. Journal of Marriage and Family. 2020. 82(1), 198-223. http://doi.org/10.1111/jomf.12646

29. Lynch KD. Advertising motherhood: Image, ideology, and consumption. Berkeley Journal of Sociololgy. 2005;49:32–57.

30. Saltman, B. Strange Situation: A mother's journey into the science of attachment. New York, Ballantine Books. 2021.

31. Cohn, LN, Pechlivanoglou, P, Lee, Y, Mahant, S, Orkin, J, Marson, A, & Cohen, E. Health outcomes of parents of children with chronic illness: a systematic review and meta-analysis. The Journal of Pediatrics. 2020. 218, 166-177. https://doi.org/10.1016/j.jpeds.2019.10.068

32. Pinquart M. Do the parent–child relationship and parenting behaviors differ between families with a child with and without chronic illness? A meta-analysis. Journal of Pediatric Psychology. 2013;38(7):708–21. http://doi.org/10.1093/jpepsy/jst020

33. DeWitt AL, Cready CM, Seward RR. Parental role portrayals in twentieth century children's picture books: More egalitarian or ongoing stereotyping? Sex Roles. 2013;69(1–2):89–106. http://doi.org/10.1007/s11199-013-0285-0

34. Schmitz, R. Constructing men as fathers: A content analysis of formulations of fatherhood in parenting magazines. The Journal of Men's studies. 2016. 24(1), 3-23. http://doi.org/10.1177/1060826515624381

35. Baird M, O'Brien M. Dynamics of parental leave in Anglophone countries: The paradox of state expansion in liberal welfare regimes. Community, Work and Family. 2015;18(2):198–217. http://dx.doi.org/10.1080/13668803.2015.1021755

36. Steinbach A. Children's and parents' well-being in joint physical custody: A literature review. Family Process. 2019;58(2):353–69. http://doi.org/10.1111/famp.12372

37. Lamb ME. Mothers, fathers, families, and circumstances: Factors affecting children's adjustment. Applied Developmental Science. 2012;16(2):98–111. https://doi.org/10.1080/10888691.2012.667344

38. Golombok S. We are family: What really matters for parents and children. London: Scribe Publications; 2020.

39. WHO. Report of the consultation on child abuse prevention 9-31 March 1999, WHO, Geneva (No. WHO/HSC/PVI/99.1). Geneva; 1999.

40. Stoltenborgh M, Bakermans-kranenburg MJ, Alink LRA, van Ijzendoorn MH. The Prevalence of child maltreatment across the globe: Review of a series of meta-analyses. Child Abuse Review. 2015;24:37–50. http://doi.org/10.1002/car.2353

41. Carr A, Duff H, Craddock F. A systematic review of reviews of the outcome of noninstitutional child maltreatment. Trauma, Violence and Abuse. 2020;21(4):828–43. https://doi.org/10.1177/1524838018801334

42. Schafer MH, Morton PM, Ferraro KF. Child maltreatment and adult health in a national sample: Heterogeneous relational contexts, divergent effects? Child Abuse & Neglect. 2014;38(3):395–406.: http://dx.doi.org/10.1016/j.chiabu.2013.08.003

43. Solomon A (2012). Far from the tree: Parents, children and the search for identity. New York: Simon and Schuster; 2012.

44. Seltzer JA, Bianchi SM. Demographic change and parent–child relationships in adulthood. Annual Review of Sociolology. 2013;39:275–90. http://doi.org/10.1146/annurev-soc-071312-145602

45. Birditt KS, Fingerman KL. Parent–child and intergenerational relationships in adulthood. In: Handbook of family theories: A content-based approach. New York: Routledge; 2013, pp. 71–86.

46. Tosi M, Albertini M. Does children's union dissolution hurt elderly parents?: Linked lives, divorce and mental health in Europe. European Journal of Population. 2019;35(4):695–717. https://doi.org/10.1007/s10680-018-9501-5

47. Fingerman KL, Cheng YP, Birditt K, Zarit S. Only as happy as the least happy child: Multiple grown children's problems and successes and middle-aged parents' well-being. Journals of Gerontology SeriesB: Psychological Sciences and Social Sciences. 2012;67 B(2):184–93. http://doi.org/10.1093/geronb/gbr086

48. Richert T, Johnson B, Svensson B. Being a parent to an adult child with drug problems: Negative Impacts on life situation, health, and emotions. Journal of Family Issues. 2018;39(8):2311–35. https://doi.org/10.1177/0192513X17748695

49. Gilligan M, Karraker A, Jasper A. Linked lives and cumulative inequality: A multigenerational family life course framework. Journal of Family Theory and Review. 2018;10(1):111–25. http://doi.org/10.1111/jftr.12244

50. Fingerman KL, Huo M, Birditt KS. Mothers, Fathers, daughters, and sons: Gender differences in adults' intergenerational ties. Journal of Family Issues. 2020;41(9):1597–625. https://doi.org/10.1177/0192513X19894369

51. David-Barrett T, Kertesz J, Rotkirch A, Ghosh A, Bhattacharya K, Monsivais D, et al. Communication with family and friends across the life course. PLoS One. 2016;11(11):1–15. http://doi.org/10.1371/journal.pone.0165687

52. Nagoski E, Nagoski A. Burnout: The secret to unlocking the stress cycle. New York: Ballantine Books; 2020.

53. Suitor JJ, Gilligan M, Peng S, Con G, Rurka M, Pillemer K. My pride and joy? Predicting favoritism and disfavoritism in mother–adult child relations. Journal of Marriage andFamily. 2016;78(4):908–25. http://doi.org/10.1111/jomf.12288

54. Vaillant GE. Triumphs of experience: The men of the Harvard Grant Study. Cambridge, MA: Harvard University Press; 2012.

55. Zartler U. Children and parents after separation. In: Research handbook on the sociology of the family. Cheltenham, UK: Edward Elgar Publishing; 2021, pp. 300–13.

56. Kalmijn M. Adult intergenerational relationships. The Wiley Blackwell companion to the sociology of families. 2014;385–403.

57. Kalmijn M. How childhood circumstances moderate the long-term impact of divorce on father–child relationships. Journal of Marriage and Family. 2015;77(4):921–38. http://doi.org/10.1111/jomf.12202

58. Agllias K. The gendered experience of family estrangement in later life. Affilia. 2013 Jul;28(3):309–21. https://doi.org/10.1177/0886109913495727

59. Birditt KS, Hartnett CS, Fingerman KL, Zarit SH, Antonucci TC. Extending the intergenerational stake hypothesis: Evidence of an intra-individual stake and implications for well-being. Journal of Marriage and Family. 2015;77(4):877–88. http://doi.org/10.1111/jomf.12203

60. Noah T. Born a crime: Stories from a South African childhood. New York: One World; 2016.

61. Kalmijn M. The effects of ageing on intergenerational support exchange: A new look at the hypothesis of flow reversal. European Journal of Population. 2019;35(2):263–84. https://doi.org/10.1007/s10680-018-9472-6

62. Lin JP, Yi CC. A comparative analysis of intergenerational relations in East Asia. International Sociology. 2013;28(3):297–315. http://doi.org/10.1177/0268580913485261

63. Canda ER. Filial piety and care for elders: A contested confucian virtue reexamined. Journal of Ethnic and Cultural Diversity in Social Work. 2013;22(3–4):213–34. https://doi.org/10.1080/15313204.2013.843134

64. Bedford O, Yeh KH. Evolution of the conceptualization of filial piety in the global context: From skin to skeleton. Frontiers in Psychology. 2021;12:1–14. https://doi.org/10.3389/fpsyg.2021.570547

65. Serrano R, Saltmana R, Yeha MJ. Laws on filial support in four Asian countries. Bulletin of the World Health Organisation. 2017;95(11):788–90.

66. Valdivieso-Mora E, Peet CL, Garnier-Villarreal M, Salazar-Villanea M, Johnson DK. A systematic review of the relationship between familism and mental health outcomes in latino population. Frontiers in Psychology. 2016;7:1–13. https://doi.org/10.3389/fpsyg.2016.01632

67. Espinoza R. The good daughter dilemma: Latinas managing family and school demands. Journal of Hispanic High Education. 2010;9(4):317–30. https://doi.org/10.1177/1538192710380919

68. Ziettlow A, Cahn N. The honor commandment: Law, religion, and the challenge of elder care. Journal of Law and Religion. 2015;30(2):229–59. https://doi.org/10.1017/jlr.2015.14

69. Rzeszut SM. The need for a stronger definition: Recognizing abandonment as a form of elder abuse across the United States. Family Court Review. 2017;55(3):444–57. https://doi.org/10.1111/fcre.12295

70. Kethineni S, Rajendran G. Elder care in the United States: Filial responsibility laws, judicial decisions, and enforcement issues. Journal of Criminal Justice and Law. 2018;2(1):68–83. https://doi.org/10.21428/b6e95092.56ca6762

71. IOM. World migration report 2020. International Organization for Migration. 2020. Available from: https://www.un.org/sites/un2.un.org/files/wmr_2020.pdf

72. Leu A, Becker S. A cross-national and comparative classification of in-country awareness and policy responses to 'young carers'. Journal of Youth Studies. 2017;20(6):750–62. https://doi.org/10.1080/13676261.2016.1260698

73. Nations U. World Population Ageing 2019 Highlights; United Nations, Department of Economic and Social Affairs. Population Division:

New York, NY, USA. 2019. Available from: https://www.un.org/en/development/desa/population/publications/pdf/ageing/WorldPopulationAgeing2019-Highlights.pdf

74. OECD. Health at a glance 2019: OECD indicators. Paris: OECD Publishing. 2019.

75. Carr D, Utz RL. Families in later life: A decade in review. Journal of Marriage and Family. 2020;82(1):346–63. https://doi.org/10.1111/jomf.12609

76. Grigoryeva A. Own gender, sibling's gender, parent's gender: The division of elderly parent care among adult children. American Sociological Review. 2017;82(1):116–46. https://doi.org/10.1177/0003122416686521

77. Miyawaki CE. A review of ethnicity, culture, and acculturation among Asian caregivers of older adults (2000–2012). SAGE Open. 2015;5(1). https://doi.org/10.1177/2158244014566365

78. Broese van Groenou MI, De Boer A. Providing informal care in a changing society. European Journal of Ageing. 2016;13(3):271–9. https://doi.org/10.1007/s10433-016-0370-7

79. Kong J, Kunze A, Goldberg J, Schroepfer T. Caregiving for parents who harmed you: A conceptual review. Clinical Gerontologist. 2021;00(00):1–13. https://doi.org/10.1080/07317115.2021.1920531

80. Anonymous. Dad has had more comebacks than Elvis: Confessions of a reluctant carer [Internet]. The Guardian. 2019. Available from: https://www.theguardian.com/lifeandstyle/2019/jan/19/dad-more-comebacks-than-elvis-confessions-of-a-reluctant-carer

81. Ooms T. The evolution of family policy: Lessons learned, challenges, and hopes for the future. Journal of Family Theory and Review. 2019;11(1):18–38. https://doi.org/10.1111/jftr.12316

82. Yon Y, Mikton CR, Gassoumis ZD, Wilber KH. Elder abuse prevalence in community settings: A systematic review and meta-analysis. The Lancet Global Health. 2017;5(2):e147–56. http://dx.doi.org/10.1016/S2214-109X(17)30006-2

83. Pillemer K, Burnes D, Riffin C, Lachs MS. Elder abuse: global situation, risk factors, and prevention strategies. The Gerontologist. 2016 Apr 1;56:194-205. https://doi.org/10.1093/geront/gnw004

84. Macfie J, Brumariu LE, Lyons-Ruth K. Parent–child role-confusion: A critical review of an emerging concept. Developmental Review. 2015;36:34–57. http://dx.doi.org/10.1016/j.dr.2015.01.002

85. Henwood M, Larkin M, Milne A, Associates MH. Seeing the wood for the trees. Carer-related research and knowledge: A scoping review. Melanie Henwood Associates. 2017. http://oro.open.ac.uk/52784/1/52784.pdf

86. Luichies I, Goossensen A, van der Meide H. Caregiving for ageing parents: A literature review on the experience of adult children. Nursing Ethics. 2019;1–20. https://doi.org/10.1177/0969733019881713

87. Bastawrous M, Gignac MA, Kapral MK, Cameron JI. Factors that contribute to adult children caregivers' well-being: A scoping review. Health and Social Care in the Community. 2015;23(5):449–66. https://doi.org/10.1111/hsc.12144

88. Reczek R, Bosley-Smith E. How LGBTQ adults maintain ties with rejecting parents: Theorizing "conflict work" as family work. Journal of Marriage and Family. 2021;43210. https://doi.org/10.1111/jomf.12765

89. Rohner RP, Lansford JE. Deep structure of the human affectional system: Introduction to interpersonal acceptance–rejection theory. Journal of Family Theory and Review. 2017;9(4):426–40. https://doi.org/10.1111/jftr.12219

90. Embleton L, Lee H, Gunn J, Ayuku D, Braitstein P. Causes of child and youth homelessness in developed and developing countries: A systematic review and meta-analysis. JAMA Pediatrics. 2016;170(5):435–44. http://doi.org/10.1001/jamapediatrics.2016.0156

91. Fazel S, Geddes JR, Kushel M. The health of homeless people in high-income countries: Descriptive epidemiology, health consequences, and clinical and policy recommendations. The Lancet. 2014;384(9953):1529–40. https://doi.org/10.1016/S0140-6736(14)61132-6

92. Agllias K. Disconnection and decision-making: Adult children explain their reasons for estranging from parents. Australian Social Work. 2016;69(1):92–104. http://dx.doi.org/10.1080/0312407X.2015.1004355

93. Scharp KM. Parent–child estrangement: Conditions for disclosure and perceived social network member reactions. Family Relations. 2016;65(5):688–700. https://doi.org/10.1111/fare.12219

94. Agllias K. Missing family: The adult child's experience of parental estrangement. Journal of Social Work Practice. 2017;0533:1–15. https://doi.org/10.1080/02650533.2017.1326471

95. Kluger J. The new science of siblings. Time. 2006. Available from: http://content.time.com/time/magazine/article/0,9171,1209949,00.html

96. Caffaro JV. Sibling abuse trauma: Assessment and intervention strategies for children, families, and adults. New York: Routledge; 2013.

97. Wolke D, Tippett N, Dantchev S. Bullying in the family: Sibling bullying. The Lancet Psychiatry. 2015;2(10):917–29. https://doi.org/10.1016/S2215-0366(15)00262-X

98. Perkins NH, Meyers A. The manifestation of physical and emotional sibling abuse across the lifespan and the need for social work intervention. Journal of Family Social Work. 2020;23(4):338–56. https://doi.org/10.1080/10522158.2020.1799894

99. Tippett N, Wolke D. Aggression between siblings: Associations with the home environment and peer bullying. Aggressive Behaviour. 2015;41(1):14–24. https://doi.org/10.1002/ab.21557

100. Dirks MA, Persram R, Recchia HE, Howe N. Sibling relationships as sources of risk and resilience in the development and maintenance of internalizing and externalizing problems during childhood and adolescence. Clinical Psychology Review. 2015;42:145–55. http://dx.doi.org/10.1016/j.cpr.2015.07.003

101. Hafford C. Sibling caretaking in immigrant families: Understanding cultural practices to inform child welfare practice and evaluation. Evaluation and Program Planning. 2010;33(3):294–302. http://dx.doi.org/10.1016/j.evalprogplan.2009.05.003

102. McKenzie Smith M, Pinto Pereira S, Chan L, Rose C, Shafran R. Impact of well-being interventions for siblings of children and young people with a chronic physical or mental health condition: A systematic review and meta-analysis. Clinical Child and Family Psychology Review. 2018;21(2):246–65. https://doi.org/10.1007/s10567-018-0253-x

103. Guterman J. Glass children. www.ted.com. 2018. Available from: https://www.ted.com/talks/jamie_guterman_glass_children

104. Caffaro JV, Conn-Caffaro A. Treating sibling abuse families. Aggression and Violent Behaviour. 2005;10(5):604–23. https://doi.org/10.1016/j.avb.2004.12.001

105. Tucker CJ, Finkelhor D. The state of interventions for sibling conflict and aggression: A systematic review. Trauma, Violence, & Abuse. 2017;18(4):396–406. https://doi.org/10.1177/1524838015622438

106. White N, Hughes C. Why siblings matter: The role of brother and sister relationships in development and well-being. London: Routledge; 2017.

107. Jenkins J, Rasbash J, Leckie G, Gass K, Dunn J. The role of maternal factors in sibling relationship quality: A multilevel study of multiple dyads per family. Journal of Child Psychology and Psychiatry. 2012;53(6):622–9. https://doi.org/10.1111/j.1469-7610.2011.02484.x

108. Buist KL, Deković M, Prinzie P. Sibling relationship quality and psychopathology of children and adolescents: A meta-analysis. Clinical Psychology Review. 2013;33(1):97–106. https://doi.org/10.1016/j.cpr.2012.10.007

109. McHale SM, Updegraff KA, Whiteman SD. Sibling relationships and influences in childhood and adolescence. Journal of Marriage and Family. 2012 Oct;74(5):913-30. https://doi.org/10.1111/j.1741-3737.2012.01011.x

110. Assink M, van der Put CE, Hoeve M, de Vries SL, Stams GJ, Oort FJ. Risk factors for persistent delinquent behavior among juveniles: A meta-analytic review. Clinical psychology review. 2015 Dec 1;42:47-61. https://doi.org/10.1016/j.cpr.2015.08.002

111. Greif G, Woolley M. Adult sibling relationships. New York. Columbia University Press; 2015 Dec 8. https://doi.org/10.7312/grei16516

112. Kowal A, Krull JL, Kramer L, Crick NR. Children's perceptions of the fairness of parental preferential treatment and their socioemotional well-being. In: Interpersonal development. London: Routledge; 2017, pp. 427–36.

113. Safer J. Cain's legacy: Liberating siblings from a lifetime of rage, shame, secrecy, and regret. New York: Basic Books; 2012.

114. Kalmijn M, Leopold T. Changing sibling relationships after parents'

death: The role of solidarity and kinkeeping. Journal of Marriage and Family. 2019;81(1):99–114. https://doi.org/10.1111/jomf.12509

115. Tanskanen AO, Danielsbacka M. Brothers and sisters across the life course: Eleven factors shaping relationship quality in adult siblings. In: Brothers and sisters. Cham: Palgrave Macmillan; 2021, pp. 25–40.

116. Steinbach A, Hank K. Full-, half-, and step-sibling relations in young and middle adulthood. Journal of Family Issues. 2018;39(9):2639–58. https://doi.org/10.1177/0192513X18757829

117. Perales F, Plage S. Sexual orientation, geographic proximity, and contact frequency between adult siblings. Journal of Marriage and Family. 2020;82(5):1444–60. https://doi.org/10.1111/jomf.12669

118. Fraley RC, Tancredy CM. Twin and sibling attachment in a nationally representative sample. Personality and Social Psychology Bulletin. 2012;38(3):308–16. https://doi.org/10.1177/0146167211432936

119. Mark KM, Pike A, Latham RM, Oliver BR. Using twins to better understand sibling relationships. Behaviour Genetics. 2017;47(2):202–14. https://doi.org/10.1007/s10519-016-9825-z

120. Strawbridge WJ, Wallhagen MI. Impact of family conflict on adult child caregivers. The Gerontologist. 1991;31(6):770–7. https://doi.org/10.1093/geront/31.6.770

121. Suitor J, Gilligan M, Johnson K, Pillemer K. Caregiving, perceptions of maternal favoritism, and tension among siblings. The Gerontologist. 2014;54(4):580–8. https://doi.org/10.1093/geront/gnt065

122. Kwak M, Ingersoll-Dayton B, Kim J. Family conflict from the perspective of adult child caregivers: The influence of gender. Journal of Social and Personal Relationships. 2012;29(4):470–87. https://doi.org/10.1177/0265407511431188

123. Witte S, Fegert JM, Walper S. Sibling relationship pattern in the context of abuse and neglect: Results from a sample of adult siblings. Child Abuse & Neglect. 2020;106:104528. https://doi.org/10.1016/j.chiabu.2020.104528

124. Wambach A. Wolfpack: How to come together, unleash our power, and change the game. London: Piatkus; 2019.

125. Angelou M. Human family: I shall not be moved. New York: Random House; 1990.

126. Thomas PA, Liu H, Umberson D. Family relationships and well-being. Innovation in Ageing. 2017;1(3):1–11. https://doi.org/10.1093/geroni/igx025

127. Wrzus C, Hänel M, Wagner J, Neyer FJ. Social network changes and life events across the life span: A meta-analysis. Psychol Bull. 2013;139(1):53–80. https://doi.org/10.1037/a0028601

128. Osher D, Cantor P, Berg J, Steyer L, Rose T. Drivers of human development: How relationships and context shape learning and development. Applied Developmental Science. 2020;24(1):6–36. https://doi.org/10.10 80/10888691.2017.1398650

129. Morris AS, Jespersen JE, Cosgrove KT, Ratliff EL, Kerr KL. Parent education: What we know and moving forward for greatest impact. Family Relations. 2020;69(3):520–42. https://doi.org/10.1111/fare.12442

130. Perry B, Winfrey O. What happened to you?: Conversations on trauma, resilience, and healing. New York: Flatiron; 2021.

131. Akhtar S, Barlow J. Forgiveness therapy for the promotion of mental well-being: A systematic review and meta-analysis. Trauma, Violence & Abuse. 2018;19(1):107–22. https://doi.org/10.1177/1524838016637079

132. Freedman S, Enright RD. The use of forgiveness therapy with female survivors of abuse. Journal of Womens Health Care. 2017;06(03). http://doi.org/10.4172/2167-0420.1000369

133. Lerner H. Why Won't You Apologize?: Healing Big Betrayals and Everyday Hurts. London, Simon and Schuster; 2017.

134. Godlewski, N. Mr. Rogers Quotes: Wisdom From the Children's Television Host on His Birthday. 3/20/18. https://www.newsweek.com/fred-rogers-birthday-quotes-wont-you-be-my-neighbor-movie-854013